D0722584

S

A

API

Expressionist Architecture in Drawings

EXPRESSIONIST ARCHITECTURE
IN DRAWINGS

Wolfgang Pehnt

 VAN NOSTRAND REINHOLD COMPANY
New York

Translated from the German
ARCHITEKTURZEICHNUNGEN DES EXPRESSIONISMUS
by John Gabriel

Copyright © 1985 by Verlag Gerd Hatje, Stuttgart

Library of Congress Catalog Card Number 84-13122

ISBN 0-442-27384-3

Printed in the German Federal Republic

Published by Van Nostrand Reinhold Company Inc.
135 West 50th Street
New York, New York 10020

Van Nostrand Reinhold
480 La Trobe Street
Melbourne, Victoria 3000, Australia

Macmillan of Canada
Division of Gage Publishing Limited
164 Commander Boulevard
Agincourt, Ontario M1S 3C7, Canada

16 15 14 13 12 11 10 9 8 7 6 5 4 3 2 1

Library of Congress Cataloging in Publication Data

Library of Congress Cataloging in Publication Data

Pehnt, Wolfgang,
  Expressionist architecture in drawings.

  Translation of: Architektur Expressionismus in
Zeichnungen.
    1. Architectural drawing – 20th century – Germany.
    2. Expressionism (Art) – Germany. I. Title.
NA2706.63P4413 1985   720'.22'2   84-13122
ISBN 0-442-27384-3

Preface

In our days an architecture that neglects materials and purpose, function and engineering and insists on the primacy of individual expression would fly in the face of modern architectural dogma. And just such an approach, whose protagonists dreamed of reshaping heaven and earth, stood at the beginning of the modern movement – or, more precisely, at one of its many beginnings, during the era of Expressionism. Architectural drawing played just as important a role during that period as it does now, though today's Post-Modernism, with its historical references, cautious precision, and intellectualism, may seem worlds apart from the stormy vitality and humanitarian zeal of the Expressionist generation.

This comparison, which reveals a few similarities and many differences, was one of the more immediate reasons for compiling a volume of this kind. Another and better reason was the sheer quality of these documents of a renewal illustrated here. Since Göran Lindahl's 1959 essay "From Cathedral of the Future to Machine for Living", since Ulrich Conrads and Hans G. Sperlich's *Fantastic Architecture* of 1960 and the overviews of Expressionist architecture written by Dennis Sharp, Borsi and König, and myself, several more specialized studies have been published on the structures and architects of Expressionism. The bequests and archives still contain undiscovered material, however, and this was yet another motive for compiling this book.

Even a slim volume like this depends on the assistance of many people. If besides the indispensable and better-known drawings I have been able to include many previously unpublished works, this would not have been possible without the cooperation of heirs and bequest administrators, collectors and museum people. My special thanks go to Mrs. Lisbet Balslev Jørgensen, Copenhagen; Mrs. Susanne Klingeberg, Itzehoe; Mrs. Marlene Charlotte Krüger, Hamburg; Mrs. Claudia Lang-Pack, Aachen; Mrs. Loretto Molzahn, Munich; Mrs. Marlene Poelzig, Hamburg; Mrs. Maria Schwarz, Cologne; Mrs. Gemma Wolters-Thiersch, Überlingen; and to Professor Gottfried Böhm, Cologne; Mr. Kasper König, Cologne; Dr. Helmut Lerch, Darmstadt; Mr. Peter Magdowski, Berlin; Dr. Winfried Nerdinger, Munich; Mr. Dieter Radicke, Berlin; Dr. Wolf Tegethoff, Kiel; Professor Oswald Mathias Ungers, Cologne; Mr. Achim Wendschuh, Berlin; Mr. Dirk van Woerkom, Amsterdam; as well as to those lenders who wished to remain anonymous, to the management and staff of the collections named in the list of plates, and to the VEB Verlag der Kunst, Dresden. It was Gerd Hatje, my publisher, who had the idea for the present book. I am particularly indebted to him and his staff, and especially to Mrs. Ruth Wurster, who shepherded the volume through all stages of production, and to Mrs. Karin Janthur for her untiring assistance in obtaining visual material.

Wolfgang Pehnt

Introduction

I.

Building is not a profession for the lone individualist. Writers, artists, and to a certain extent composers and sculptors, can do most of their work alone in the studio, but architects depend on the cooperation of many other people – clients, contractors, builders, engineers, officials, financing experts and real estate agents. And if they want to communicate some special message with their work, they have to explain it to all concerned. Nor is the fact that they are tremendously moved by their own vision any guarantee that the other people involved will be. Architects who create, as Bruno Taut put it, "out of a strong emotion" and whose buildings are meant to speak "to the emotions only"[1] thus face much greater difficulties than artists in other fields when it comes to finding acceptance for unfamiliar ideas. The Expressionist architects never felt completely at home in three-dimensional reality. They were able to execute their projects only under the most favourable circumstances – where architects' dreams met with such high public receptiveness as they did in Amsterdam, where a community of philosophic interest existed as in Dornach, or where an experimentally-minded patron commissioned a private residence, as happened here and there during the 1910s and early 1920s.

But seated at the drawing board, these architects with a message were absolutely free. They could envisage crystal domes, bridges between Alpine peaks, skyscraping cities and human-oriented settlements regardless of the division of labour and its strictures. Only when they were content to rule over a sheet of paper were architects truly kings, those "leaders and masters of the visual artists"[2] and farsighted shapers of human destiny that they imagined themselves to be during the Expressionist years. Pencil and charcoal, pen and brush enabled them to capture, far from the compulsions of the building site, every passing fancy and heartfelt wish. If Expressionist architecture existed more on paper than in three-dimensional reality, it was because drawing is the medium that offers least resistance to imaginative vision.

It was no disadvantage in the eyes of their contemporaries that architects should depend so strongly on the tools of fine art. Though the architects may have claimed priority, declaring that their art was the mother of all, even some of their sharpest critics recommended that they limit themselves to drawing and sketching as a beneficial means of self-reflection. This was the only way in which the art of building could repair the link with the other arts which all too much utilitarian thinking had shattered. "If present-day architecture is almost completely cut off from the extremely vital efforts being made in sculpture and painting," wrote Paul Westheim in 1919, "if it can fructify just as little in that direction as it can receive new impetus in return, the reason may well be that intense building activity has caused it to lose touch with its true basis".[3] A temporary return to the means of two-dimensional art (or, in the case of architectural models, to the means of sculpture) was recommended as a rite of initiation to the insights that painters and sculptors had already achieved.

During the 1920s such insights were labelled Expressionist, and architecture began to be measured against the works of Expressionist painters and sculptors. Was architecture indeed an "emanation of indomitable personality", a "radiation of the spirtit" involving "creative audactiy", "imagina-

tive experience", and a "boiling over of sensibility"[4]? "The creative art of building", enthused Westheim, "is just as much an imaginative projection into materials of humanity, intelligence, power and grandeur as is creation in paint or clay, the translation of a higher idea of the universe into artistic reality, the infusion of an inner musical rhythm into space and stone; it means dreaming and dream-shaping, that same ineffable, titanic, insatiable passion which attempted to rage itself out in both Rembrandt and Michelangelo."[5] Westheim's no less enthusiastic colleague Walter Müller-Wulckow drew the uncontrovertible conclusion that this passion was "bound to lead to an Expressionism that will seem unusual in architecture for some time to come"[6].

Where the creative urge was so highly valued, the architectural sketch became doubly significant. Sketches promised insight into the creative process, and with their aid artists could tap sources that would otherwise remain buried. Expressionism banked on spontaneity and intuition, not on results achieved through involvement and compromises with reality. "The recording of a vision is so infinitely more important than the trimming down and pruning out required to meet actual conditions ... Because these sudden pyrotechnic bursts of genius illuminate in a flash the depths where the Inconceivable lies."[7] Drawings were also expected to point to the tasks of the future. Not only were they conceived as opening channels to the primal source of all creative power, they were a challenge to the imagination: "An architectural sketch continually restimulates the imagination, making it help work, help build, help *will*", declared Adolf Behne in the brochure for an exhibition of drawings.[8] The unfinished character of architectural sketches was considered a guarantee of their openness to the future – a utopian quality that existed independently of the utopian subject represented.

It is not surprising that exhibitions of architects' drawings burgeoned during the first months and years after World War I. In April 1919, the Berlin Arbeitsrat für Kunst (Working Council for Art) organized an "Exhibition for Unknown Architects", followed in May 1920 by "New Building". The artists' society Novembergruppe, also of Berlin and closely allied with the Arbeitsrat, included architects' designs, drawings, models and photographs in their shows as a matter of course. The Paul Cassirer gallery, at Henry van de Velde's suggestion, exhibited in 1919 the sketches that Erich Mendelsohn had made during the war and recast the year after. Sections were devoted to architecture at other regularly scheduled events such as the Dresden Secession and Grosse Berliner Kunstausstellung. In Amsterdam, the group Architectura et Amicitia held many exhibitions, of which their 1915 show, with Michel de Klerk, Johan Melchior van der Mey, and Piet Kramer, must have looked like a demonstration of Dutch Expressionists. The organizers of events like these appealed to a different and more committed audience than that of normal art shows. "To a much higher degree than non-applied art," wrote Adolf Behne, "architectural designs appeal to the *will* and thus fulfil a mission."[9] People who appreciated these drawings of a future architecture were considered allies, who were willing to accept more responsibility than the normal buyer and collector of art and who participated in the development of the new work of the building art from the beginning.

Designs produced by Expressionist architects during this period seldom disappointed these high expectations. In

6

Max Pechstein(?). Flysheet for the *Arbeitsrat für Kunst* (Working Council for Art). 1919

Hans Poelzig's drawings, surfaces roughed in with charcoal or wash evoke a primordial layer out of which identifiable shapes and spaces begin to emerge. Ornamental sequences, striving upward in pointed gothic spires or outward in forceful baroque arabesques, mark off a dancing rhythm in which the separate beats are linked into space-defining chains. The violence of these images suggests the rapidity with which they must have appeared to Poelzig's mind's eye. Speaking of his studies for a Festival Hall in Salzburg, Poelzig once recalled that a "more or less mild frenzy" had seized him when he saw the natural theatre at Mirabell and Hellbrunn, driving every thought from his mind except "how to supplement, or even surpass, this world of form with something essentially related".[10] In the case of Hans Scharoun, such conjurings-up of spirits took on an explosive character. His sheaves of form lick like flames, shoot like crystals, or break like exotic fruits out of the earth; the streamlined shapes of the somewhat later drawings, like strange creatures made of some unknown kind of protoplasm, rush as if from afar into the rectangle of the paper. In Rudolf Schwarz's drawings a knotted and tangled network of energy-charged lines shape themselves into the facades of sacred buildings. An indefinite spatial depth is evoked simultaneously with volume, as though the structures brought the atmosphere out of which they have materialized along with them.

In works such as those of Poelzig and Schwarz (his former master-student), those of Jefim Golyscheff, and certain of Hermann Finsterlin's drawings, definition of space and volume appears to have been achieved by letting the hand move of its own accord. This spontaneous gestural automatism prefigures Surrealist techniques of visual evocation. Moreover, these are the drawings that evince most clearly two further traits of the Expressionist approach to architecture: an extremely close, reciprocal relationship between interior and exterior space, and the independence of Expressionist designs from their material realization. The first aspect, an interdependence of interior and exterior that dissolves the solid walls of traditional architecture, has since become a prime criterion of all modern architecture. The early, Expressionist version of this integration, however, employed means different from those of the later, classical modern. Instead of articulating space in terms of clearly defined structural elements – point-like sections, precise planes, and platonic volumes – the Expressionists conceived both spaces and solid bodies as a plastically modelled continuum. In Poelzig's sketches, the earth bulges into configurations that

may appear either organic or man-made, function as enclosing shell or enclosed sculpture, cavern or tower. Many of Finsterlin's drawings show eroded, jagged formations projecting and impinging – glacial landscapes which the eyes traverses without being able to tell us whether we are on ice or solid ground. Of course, besides these geomorphic approaches other compositional techniques offered themselves, techniques derived from Cubism in which the synthesis of interior and exterior space could be expressed in groupings of overlapping and superimposed fragments of form.

As with exterior and interior space, it is impossible in many of these drawings to distinguish beween organic nature and the results of human intervention. In Wenzel August Hablik's early drawings, man seems to have burrowed into the crystallizations of a primordial world, continuing to shape them as if the human imagination were an anonymous force of nature. Bruno Taut interpreted the intervention of man the building animal among the Alpine peaks as the work of some demiurgic jeweller who, carefully facetting and polishing, lent ores and minerals a beauty characterized by strange mergers of the as-yet-unformed with the already formed. In a sketch for his album *Alpine Architecture,* the main nave of a "Cliff Cathedral" overtops a narrow chasm while its aisles merge with caves and grottoes chipped out of the mountainside, reversing positive and negative form. The ambiguity of this technique of representation is paralleled by the ambiguity of its content.

These suggestions and borderline ambiguities are complicated by the fact that the means of material realization, beyond the drawing, have seldom been taken into consideration. Materials are indeed sometimes specified in *Alpine Architecture* and Finsterlin's "Wohnlinge", but the bridges and piers of emerald green or ruby red glass, the crystal needles of the mountaintops, the frosted glass domes and arbitrarily tinted concrete shells, the porphyry boulders, ebony structures, gilded copper roofs, and silver-plated columns were evidently meant to evoke costliness, brilliancy and colour rather than as practical construction specifications. Interestingly, it was a man untrained in architecture who devoted most thought to the realization of his utopian schemes. Wenzel August Hablik, in his designs for self-supporting cupolas and exhibition towers erected on staggered, polygonal plans, took account of such practical problems as scaffolding, wind forces and snow loads. But in many other drawings of this period, the architects appear to have relied on some infinitely malleable substance to help them in the play of metamorphoses. No such material was available on the market, of course, nor has it been invented since.

Another technique of representation that answered well to the quid pro quo of space and sculpture was a development and ramification of basic forms in seemingly endless series. Erich Mendelsohn used to sketch out morphological sequences with great rapidity (and with stimulating gramophone music in the background). Finsterlin's work includes drawings that almost systematically investigate the potentialities of an embryonal shape, frequently crossing the borderline into figurative, even sometimes physiognomic interpretations. Yet such first, shorthand notes, attempts to record an idea that has not developed into complex figuration, have less of the specific tone of the period than other, more finished drawings. There is an Expressionism of the moment that is found not only in the works of the Expressionists. Gradually working up to and pinning down an idea in sketch after sketch is something architects have practised whenever a notebook, the back of an envelope, or a paper napkin fell into their hands – an occupational habit and also a bit of prestidigitation that is good for one's status consciousness and part of the architectural game.

There was too much diversity of temperament among Expressionist architects to allow them to be subsumed under a unified aesthetic. If some of them seemed to develop their ideas in the process of sketching, letting the pencil glide across the paper of its own accord, other artists obviously had the finished structure in mind before they began to draw. And they worked out such conceptions to various degrees of finish. Erich Mendelsohn set his ideas down in pregnant contours and enlarged his original, tiny sketches "like poster roughs", as Walter Curt Behrendt rather deprecatingly put it. [11] Many of Finsterlin's ideas congealed in a calligraphic shorthand, while Otto Bartning recorded his hesitatingly, and with an almost anxious precision.

The differing states of these aggregates of form were not only a function of the artists' personal idiosyncrasies. They were also determined by opportunities for realization of the designs and thus by the purpose for which the drawings were made. Where it was a matter of dimensioning and structural reconsideration as in many of Michel de Klerk's sketches, or where the client had to be provided with a lucid view of his future real estate, the spontaneous gesture was out of place. The rendering as a means of communicating an idea to others demanded a different approach from the monologue of the rapid sketch. Still different means were required by the educational and moral aims that members of Bruno Taut's circle pursued. Taut himself, not an extraordinarily gifted draughtsman, frequently resorted to multiple views in his depictions, combinations of elevation and ground plan, overall view and detail, a juxtaposition of characteristic parts of the building accompanied by exhaustive commentary. This combination of lettering and image was among the typical visual means of the period. Concerned foremost with dramatic effects, the Expressionists placed little weight on purity of genre. Making one's message understood was the prime thing, and hence Taut's or Hablik's drawings explain their authors' intentions in words and pictures that recall popular illustrated sheets or even the comic strips that had just begun to appear at the time.

The closer architects were to an actual commission, the less subjective their methods became. The archives of the Amsterdam architects, for instance, contain relatively few drawings in which the furies of the subconscious have been allowed free rein. These men adapted their fantasies to realisable buildings, while many of their German counterparts considered drawing an end in itself. With the Dutch architects a sketch was often a descriptive prediction of some imaginative reality; with the Germans, it was that reality itself.

II.

The period immediately following World War I was a time of great deprivation for everyone in defeated Germany, but for the architects it meant facing special professional problems. Practising architecture during the first postwar years amounted to managing shortages and dealing with need. The construction business profited least of all branches of trade from the inflationary tendencies of the market. When the government saw itself compelled to administrate housing, private investors lost interest in the housing field. A scarcity of raw materials – particularly losses in coal production capacity – runaway building prices, and high interest rates on capital prevented investment in other areas of building as well. As the letters of Bruno Taut and Walter Gropius testify, even established architects often faced acute problems in making a living.

In these conditions, the sketchbook offered a substitute for non-existent commissions, and publication or exhibition were the only ways to disseminate ideas in the absence of built architecture. Bruno Taut's 1919 and 1920 initiatives as spokesman of the younger generation were all on paper – that exchange of graphic and written ideas he encouraged among his friends and that later came to be known as Gläserne Kette; his project for a musical drama, *Der Weltbaumeister*; and his planned film, whose scenes were to be designed and drawn by his Gläserne Kette correspondents. These drawings, done without any hope of practical realization, informed by utopian idealism, and, as in Taut's portfolios, predicated on the emergence of a new audience, a populace reconciled with art, were a product of unemployed years. Taut's great hope was that his and his friends' architectural visions would strike "aspiring workingmen" with the imaginative force of art. "When you say they have, brothers," he wrote, "we will be gratified beyond words. It will show us that you are prepared to help us build, and convince us that the early dawn of a new culture is already emerging on the horizon." [12]

During the years – or was it only months? – when a spiritual and cultural revolution still seemed possible, many latent developments appeared to be coming to a head. Even the term "Expressionism" harked back to a pre-1914 movement. In painting, this stylistic label had found currency in the course of 1911; it was first applied to architecture about a year later by Adolf Behne, who was always quick to spot new trends. Writing about the work of Bruno Taut in the journal *Pan* for 1912-13, Behne obviously still felt that much justification was required for calling an activity so strongly dependent on real conditions "Expressionist". Expressionist in the deepest sense, he stated, was whatever "emerged solely from inside". A waiver of preconceived notions of order, an intense involvement with every new challenge, and forms that were "truly inspired, truly organic" were for him unfailing signs of the new attitude. [13]

But had not such "truly inspired, truly organic" forms only recently been achieved, in Art Nouveau and Jugendstil, only to be rejected as ostentatious, arbitrary and artsy-craftsy? The first decade of the century had seen a neo-classical revival in Germany, a return to late-eighteenth century art that practised a Goethean serenity in domestic architecture and translated the requirements of the machine age into a new brand of industrial classicism. Part of its adherents' strategy was to represent the ideas and products of Art Nouveau as belonging to the past, a *fin de siècle* rather than a new beginning, the swan-song of a doomed era. Certain historians, who simplified their task by assuming that history was a linear process, lent support to this view by hindsight. But the impulse of the Nineties was much too strong and the modern movement much too full of promise for it to succumb so easily. In many regions of Europe – Finland, Scotland, and Catalonia especially – Art Nouveau had been more than a passing style; it had contributed to the forma-

Otto Kohtz. From *Gedanken über Architektur* (Thoughts on Architecture). Berlin, 1909

tion of a national or regional identity. Achievements of this scope are not discarded lightly. Catalonian Modernisme, for instance, could not have been less concerned with art-historical boundaries. Long after Art Nouveau had been buried by general agreement, Puig i Cadafalch, Josep M. Jujol, and above all Antoni Gaudí went on contributing to their region's modernist architecture with its characteristic amalgam of traditional brick construction, Gothic and northern Arabian ornament, and international modern influence. This "Neo-Catalonian" style was known to the Expressionist generation of architects in Central Europe thanks to a few, scattered publications. Hermann Finsterlin even corresponded with Gaudí, and Walter Gropius visited him during a trip to Spain in 1908. [14]

Though Art Nouveau prepared the ground for Expressionism in its use of architectural forms to convey significance and emotion, the biomorphic tendencies of early Art Nouveau found only partial acceptance among the younger generation. Wherever organically inspired shapes occur in the work, say, of Finsterlin, Mendelsohn, or Rudolf Steiner, the Expressionist penchant for the hard and crystalline has generally led them to choose the skeletons of living things as models — branches of coral, snail or mussel shells, and bone structures. But more importantly, the "expressive ornament" of Art Nouveau had already well-nigh explored the capacity of architectural configurations for conveying "the whole range of human feeling and states of mind — joy and pain, waking and dreaming, weakness and power", as Walter Curt Behrendt has written. [15]

These similarities being what they were, it is no wonder that contacts across the generations came about. The organizers of the Exhibition for Unknown Architects invited Hermann Obrist, the visionary but almost completely forgotten sculptor and Art Nouveau ornament designer, to participate in their 1919 show. Erich Mendelsohn quite frankly admired both Obrist and Henry van de Velde, who for his part called Mendelsohn his only true pupil. *Wendingen*, the organ of the Amsterdam Expressionists, devoted long articles and even entire special issues to such pioneers as Jan Toorop, Koloman Moser, Gustav Klimt, and Josef Hoffmann. Michel de Klerk, the boy genius of the Amsterdam school, which began earlier than its German counterpart and was thus closer in time to Art Nouveau, took many of his motifs from the English and Scottish or Austro-German branches of the

movement. That incunabulum of the Expressionist art of building, Bruno Taut's glass pavilion at the 1914 Cologne Werkbund Exhibition, contained a showcase full of the fragile, shimmering creations of Louis Comfort Tiffany — a younger man's homage to a forerunner who, like him, was out to create a *Gesamtkunstwerk*. Taut's critics argued accordingly, accusing him of regressing into a past that had long been overcome.

The idea of a total work of art, which Art Nouveau attempted to realize in terms of an aesthetic ensemble and the Expressionists in terms of a social unity, included the reshaping of the natural environment. No less than a perfection of the entire visible world was what it implied. Neither Paul Scheerbart's literary fantasies — one of the Expressionist architects' sacred texts — nor the graphic utopias of Hablik and Bruno Taut stopped short of visions of terrestrial, even cosmic redesign. Now, it is one of the paradoxes of expansive thinking that the larger its plans, the smaller the scale of their visualization tends to be — a sheet of drawing paper is the utopian's true medium. This tradition of visionary drawing, too, stretched back unbroken into the days of Art Nouveau. The students of Otto Wagner or Hermann Billing (who had trained Hans Luckhardt and Max Taut) dreamed of mysterious mergings of nature with the works of man. They envisioned lonely temples accessible to only a few adepts, the

Hermann Billing. Architectural Sketch. 1903. From *Architektur-Skizzen* (Architectural Sketches). Stuttgart, n. d. (1904)

9

elect who bore Zarathustra's message in their hearts, high above precipitous chasms, and set the enigmatic eyes of human habitations in forbidding mountain peaks. The work of Hablik, who was fascinated from the beginning by mountain architecture and crystalline forms, provides the clearest evidence of a link across the generations from Art Nouveau to Arbeitsrat and the group around Bruno Taut. Hablik's creative experience reached back to the turn of the century, when he studied at the Vienna School of Arts and Crafts, and these memories remained a catalyst in his work right down through the postwar period.

"An idea moved mountains – one thundering word blasted stars out of their orbits and, as if with arms of godlike power, gripped deep, deep into infinite space – creating, shaping, with intractable eternal force." [16] The words are Hablik's, but all the utopian architects experienced their individual creative power in such demigod-like terms. Artists, they believed, were active creators and vessels of inspiration in one, both weak and strong, both servants and masters of art. In this notion of the lone genius called to renew the world, they were of a mind with Nietzsche. The philosopher was one of their prophets; another was Paul Scheerbart, the teller of tales. From Nietzsche they drew their pathos, their trust in the sacredness of the visible and tangible world, their belief that a Dionysian age was imminent, their horror of middle-class complacency and state paternalism, and their faith in the creative act as a transporting experience. Scheerbart represented the down-to-earth, witty antipode to Nietzsche, predicting that once his architecture of glass and crystal became a reality, a new ethic would arise. His eccentric novels also contained such practical tips for architects as this: "If you intend to build in comparatively large dimensions, it is to be recommended that the natural environment be used such that the final result looks as if you had created the existing environment along with the rest. It is generally agreed that stylizing expanses of cliff is of higher value to an architect than erecting the usual four-walled buildings", Paul Scheerbart assures us already in a novel of 1900. [17]

What distinguished the utopian Expressionists from their Art Nouveau predecessors was their social commitment. Most of the architects among them professed a universal socialism beyond all party squabbles, a "spiritual community" without which, according to Wijdeveld, no general principle of style could emerge. [18] The reform movements of the pre-war period and the vanguard artists' groups of the war and postwar years, with their pacifist, anarchist and activist politics, lent new meaning to the repertoire of Art Nouveau form they had inherited. Instead of addressing themselves to a select congregation gathered to celebrate an aesthetic cult, they were out to win over the entire population. In 1903, Obrist had said that with all due respect for folk art, fine art was a different thing, and that this luxury was a mental and material cultural necessity. On the contrary, Adolf Behne, reflecting on the relation of art to society a decade and a half later, reserved his praise for artists who found the source of all creative power in the people. "There can be no question", Behne wrote, "that the masses, and only the masses, still lead an uncorrupted, fruitful, independent life. This stratum alone is conceivable as the vehicle of a coming culture, because it alone is virgin land, unadulterated soil." [19] The Expressionist groups waxed euphoric both about the people as an audience and also about its artistic products. Thus the Berlin Arbeitsrat für Kunst advertised in newspapers in the hope of discovering anonymous talents and encouraging popular participation in their programmes. Such exalted aims were not, however, backed up by practical political involvement, either among the German Expressionists or their Dutch counterparts, though Amsterdam Expressionism would hardly have been conceivable without the Social Democratic climate of that city and the housing programmes of the SDAP. As far as Expressionists were concerned, all political parties were moribund and the State was a relic of nationalist prestige thinking.

With social idealism and pacifism two types of building projects took on special importance, the *Volkshaus* or community centre and the religious building in the widest sense. Community centres had been planned and in a few cases even erected before the war, particularly in government housing developments. In 1911, for example, the German Werdandi Society held a competion for an estate with community centre, stipulating that this building was to occupy the middle of the site and was to include an auditorium, a swimming pool, and various shops. At the height of the war, in 1917, a *Volkshaus* Society was founded to put up community centres that would double as war memorials. Among the high-minded Expressionists, projects of this kind took on a truly cultic aspect, being exalted to crystal domes and palaces designed not only to cater to the inhabitants' mundane needs but to serve as places of meditation in a worldly religion. They called their shrines of shining crystal "cathedrals of humanity" where the transformed human beings of the future could purge their souls. "A Meeting Place of Nations" was the theme of a competition organized in 1919 by *Shivsculptarch,* the Soviet commission for a synthesis of painting, sculpture and architecture, and its results were shown in Moscow the following year. Bruno Taut's temple projects, by contrast, were meant for the individual, as places of self-communion and solitary meditation.

Nor was the older generation immune to the prevailing mood. During the war years in neutral Holland, Berlage designed a "Pantheon of Humanity", sited on a hill with eight avenues leading up to it. The inner sanctum, watched over by towers of Love and Courage, Inspiration and Prudence, Science and Power, Liberty and Peace, and surrounded by courtyards of quiet contemplation, was intended as a monument to the unity of mankind. Berlage flanked this central hall with galleries of Memory and Reconciliation, and spanned it with a dome of International Community. Younger architects scoffed at the rather heavy-handed allegory of this pantheon, though really its pathos was only a more rational variant of their own cult of crystal. This pathos continued to inform Berlage's work as late as his 1926 project for a Lenin Mausoleum.

When those who built churches for the established faiths expressed their longing for sacred spaces, they did so in terms not much different from those employed by architects who conceived crystal cathedrals for some unknown religion. A pious person, said Otto Bartning, "finds his way to church out of a conscious or unconscious need to immerse his ego in the great melting pot of the community – in the hope not only to unite his voice with a thousand other voices in the same words but to lend his outcry from the depths of despair a thousand tongues and a thousand mouths." [20] Ecclesiastical architecture seemed to provide the great communal task that many had longed for, bringing the idea of a total work of art closer to realization and, moreover, promising contact with the masses. Thus Adolf Behne could see the church building as "the form assumed by a tremendous emotion that unites the multitude".[21] The church designs of both Protestant and Catholic architects favoured a unified space in which private acts of devotion were secondary to services that included the entire congregation. Within the Catholic Church, this idea was championed by the Liturgical Movement, while such Protestant architects as Otto Bartning advocated what they termed "unanimous space". In both cases, the exalted emotions and ideals typical of the period were bound up with actual projects, which is why visionary thinking remained vital for a longer time in this field of architecture than in any other. Bartning, Dominikus Böhm, Rudolf Schwarz and many other ecclesiastical architects were still translating visions into reality long after the ecstatic reawakening elsewhere had succumbed to disillusion.

For both kinds of task, religious building and community centre, Gothic was an obvious model. This needs no explanation in the case of church architecture – besides Romanesque, Gothic had been the prime stylistic ideal of the nineteenth century. Gothic forms would still answer to modern needs, architects felt, if only they were divested of archaeological pedantry and infused with high emotion. And the community spirit, integrating force, and religious strength associated with the Gothic style could also be extended to those buildings which were to provide a new focus for the temporal community. "The architect's ideal building, the community centre," wrote Paul Wolf, "will set the dominant accent, a cathedral of the future, in the residential

Sigismund Vladislavovich Dombrovski. Meeting-place of the Peoples. 1919

cities to come."[22] Indeed the notion of a "cathedral of socialism", which got the Weimar Bauhaus into great political trouble, crops up just as often in the writings of the period as the idea of a revived *Bauhütte,* a guild of pious and devoted artisans who, "longing for community, make one last attempt to reach out for heaven".[23] Among art critics and historians, those who paved the way for a contemporary reception of the Gothic style were particularly Wilhelm Worringer in *Abstraktion und Einfühlung* (1908) and Karl Scheffler in *Geist der Gotik* (1917).

Gothic was seen as an embodiment of creative labour in which an isolation of architectural elements was just as unknown as an isolation of artists and craftsmen from one another or from their community. Its forms were so moving, Behne wrote, because we are always aware that "besides this one gem, many other, equally beautiful and equally inexhaustible ones gleam, and that they are all solidly set in the strong, supple and grand body of space", and his words applied not only to forms but to convictions and feelings as well.[24] In terms of a synthesis of all the arts, the Baroque might have provided as good a model as the Gothic. A Baroque formal exuberance indeed echoes in many of the designs of the day, particularly in those of Hans Poelzig, who as City Architect in Dresden and planner of the Salzburg Festival buildings worked in two strongholds of the Baroque style. But the Expressionist generation as a whole found the Baroque imagination lacking in the "sublime aims of the Gothic will; tranquillity, contemplation, and nearness to God were foreign to it. Ruled by the same blind and everlasting drive, its flame shot outwards, while the flame of Gothic had burned inwardly."[25]

A still brighter light, however, shone beyond the confines of the Western world – *ex oriente lux*. Behind the Gothic cathedral shimmered an apparition of the Indian temple. "Is not India much *more* than Gothic?" asked Adolf Behne. Authors of the day, though most of them had seen the wonders of the East only in photographs, found no superlative too strong when it came to describing them. "One can hardly say where art begins in the monuments of India, with such abundance, such breadth, such ease do they grow out of the whole, out of the ponds, rivers and mountains, out of the sunlight, the land, the countless hands and hearts. They can be separated from the life of the populace as little as a living brain can be cut off from the blood circulating in all the body's arteries."[26] The Asiatic themes of Expressionist poetry and such movements of philosophical renewal as theosophy are records of the fascination exerted, in the words of Theodor Däubler, by the "sensual presence of far lands across the sea".[27] Stupa and pagoda, opulent domes and swarming detail left their mark on Western architects' drawings and on some of the few structures that were actually built during those years. Dutch architects, at least, could fall back on the first-hand knowledge of the East provided by their country's colonies. Their graphic and decorative work in particular often echoes the fantastic planar patterning of Indonesian art.

III.

An architecture that shifted the relationship of function to form strongly in favor of form, subordinating every other consideration to expressive shapes and emotional appeals, emerged almost simultaneously in many parts of Europe. And as in Central Europe, these movements' plans to change the face of the earth, a missionary zeal inherited from turn-of-the-century reform movements, Art Nouveau, and Secessionism, seldom got off the drawing board. The Italian Futurists would have liked to transform the world into a dynamic totality, a gigantic urban machine. The Czech Cubists, who were at least able to bring a number of their projects to fruition, combined memories of Bohemian Gothic with the latest pictorial formulas imported from Paris, developing an expressive approach opposed to the dogma of Vienna, the headquarters of the Austro-Hungarian Empire. During its first project phase, Russian revolutionary architecture achieved ecstatic configurations that came very close to those of the Central European Expressionists, though they soon gave way to the technological pathos of Soviet modernism.

Many biographical and organizational crosslinks existed between these movements and Expressionism in the stricter sense. Despite a recognizable common impulse, however, their formal repertoires deserve to be defined independently. The existing stylistic categories are simply not flexible enough to clearly distinguish the various streams and do justice to their significance. The hypothetical term "Expressionist Architecture", in other words, can be construed more or less liberally depending on whether one's aim is to cover as many relevant phenomena as possible or achieve the greatest possible focus. In this book the selection of drawings has been limited to German and Dutch artists. Contemporaries applied the term "Expressionist" to both.

Vlatislav Hofman. Study for a Tombstone. 1913

As might have been expected from their related language, relations were very close between groups of architects and artists in Holland and Germany. Hendrik Petrus Berlage figured not only as the doyen of Dutch architecture (at least until he unmistakably distanced himself from the 1920s vanguard), but of the modern movement itself – that "solid cliff in a restless sea", as Bruno Taut characterized him.[28] The journal *Wendingen,* around which the Dutch Expressionists congregated, maintained close contacts with Germany. The "worthy inn of Wendingen", as Hermann Finsterlin affectionately named it,[29] devoted special issues to both Finsterlin and Erich Mendelsohn. Bruno Taut's *Architekturprogramm* of 1918, his book *Die Stadtkrone,* and his magazine *Frühlicht* were read and discussed in Holland, if not without critical reservations. In the eyes of Jan Frederik Staal, Taut's book offered not too much but too little utopia: "We in this tame country of flat, rectangular fields between straight, shallow ditches hope, hope for anything that might relieve this monotony and foment a revolt against this parcelled-out, flat world (a bit of land for me, a bit of land for you) – we hope in our tranquil but oh so confined bay for at least a breeze from the storm that heaves the limitless ocean beyond our borders." Hoping this much, Staal concluded: "A light, a torch, Taut's book is not."[30] In 1923, Taut gave a lecture before Architectura et Amicitia, as did Erich Mendelsohn.

It was particularly Hendrikus Theodorus Wijdeveld, the chief editor of *Wendingen* and hence a spokesman for Dutch Expressionism, who maintained ties with Germany, ties that had been prepared not lastly by the architect J. L. Mathieu Lauweriks, who lived and taught in western Germany for many years.[31] Sketches by Wijdeveld have survived which he made of Hans Poelzig's Grosses Schauspielhaus in Berlin. He himself was working at the time on a project for a popular theatre, part of an extensive complex in the Vondelpark in Amsterdam. Adolf Behne, who travelled in Holland in 1920 and intended to put on an exhibition of Dutch architects at the Berlin Arbeitsrat für Kunst, quoted Wijdeveld's description of the young Amsterdam artist-architects verbatim – those "rogues and incendiaries of the architectural profession" who "dance like satyrs around the hot smoking coals of the masses, singing a song of liberation".[32]

German architects kept a close eye on developments in the Amsterdam School. Otto Bartning, who had also been to Holland, praised their "structures growing from earth to rooftop, soaring from one end to the other, radiating from interior to exterior; space emerging effortlessly from space, volume generating, impelling, ascending on volume".[33] The fact that the architecture of De Stijl was emerging as an antipode to this, as Bartning put it, "expression of a spontaneous will, a passionate growth" seemed to the German architect to promise a future synthesis. Simplicity stood opposed to complexity, Cubist clarity to dynamic force, cool-headed rationality to the spark of intuition; and the two poles would exert a mutual attraction that could only lead to a great reconciliation. This respect for the achievements of the Amsterdam School remained strong even after developments in Holland, as in Germany, had been diverted into different channels. As late as 1929, Bruno Taut could still call it a miracle that collective architecture had emerged there "in which the individual house was no longer important but long rows of houses concentrated into streets, which

Nikolai Ivanovich Iszelenov. Meeting place of the Peoples. 1919

in turn were concentrated into a larger unity, even though many architects had worked on them".[34]

While in Germany the Expressionists' formal daring was manifested without compromise only in certain, scattered structures – churches, a handful of apartment blocks, Poelzig's Grosses Schauspielhaus, Erich Mendelsohn's early work, Rudolf Steiner's fortress of anthroposophy at Dornach near Basel, and in Bernhard Hoetger's completed projects – the buildings of the Amsterdam School were almost too numerous to count. It is true that these "graceful architectonic sculptures that follow the cadences of developing space in full swing" (Wijdeveld)[35] were concentrated on certain quarters of Amsterdam such as Spaarndammer Buurt and the southern and western parts of the city. But many were located in other sections as well, and their influence was felt throughout the country. After beginning with Willem Kromhout's pioneering work, after the designs produced by the emerging Amsterdam School during the first decade of the century, after Michel de Klerk's Hillehuis in Amsterdam and Piet Kramer's Sailors' Union in Den Helder, both of which were erected in 1911–12, Amsterdam Expressionism first culminated in the Scheepvaarthuis designed by the architect trio of Johan Melchior van der Mey, de Klerk, and Kramer (1912–16). The full-blown Expressionist style lasted almost two decades in Holland. Not only did it begin earlier and unfold more freely in Holland than in Germany, but it was destined to be longer-lived.

This relative constancy, something the style did not enjoy in other countries, had organizational reasons. In 1916 the progressives took over the helm of Architectura et Amicitia, the Dutch association of architects. Not only the crucial municipal building boards but the government department of works, the Rijksgebouwendienst, came to be headed by affiliates of the Amsterdam School who obtained commissions for its members, or sometimes even built in its style themselves. Thus Piet Kramer was entrusted with the design of no less than 400 bridges in the course of the city's adaptation to increasing automobile traffic. The committees to beautify Amsterdam, responsible for approving the facade of every building erected on municipal property, were also staffed by *Wendingen* affiliates after the war, and they proved to be powerful instruments of that group's interests. Any contractor who wanted to be sure of obtaining a committee's approval was well advised to employ an architect who worked in the *Wendingen* style.

The exotic brickwork of the Amsterdam School had its critics nonetheless. Its expense was a main point of contention from an early date, and the postwar housing shortage, more serious than ever, fueled the debate. Yet as long as fine craftsmanship and artistic inventiveness continued to be the pride of the workmen who lived there, the style was able to hold its ground. De Klerk was indeed an expensive architect, admitted F. M. Wibaut, the Social Democratic deputy for Amsterdam public housing. But de Klerk did not build too expensively, he added, because that was something an extraordinary artist could never do.

This epoch in Amsterdam came to an end about the middle of the 1920s. Expressionist housing projects now began to be valued aesthetically as what in many cases they had always been structurally – a masquerade, with imaginative facades grafted like false fronts onto the run-of-the-mill plans of private contractors and building companies. In 1923, when private housing got a stronger support, a profit-conscious clientele came into being who were no longer willing to finance the exuberance of High Expressionist ar-

J. L. Mathieu Lauweriks. Design for the title-page of *Wendingen*, issue of January 1918

13

chitecture. The death of Michel de Klerk, the great magician of the Amsterdam group – he died in late 1923 – marked the end of an era in many people's eyes. Both *Architectura* and *Wendingen* devoted special memorial issues to him.

In Germany, too, where important commissions had had to wait until the inflation was over, the vanguard set out to explore new shores. Expressionist building had never been as firmly anchored there as in Holland. The pressing need to economize, experiments in industrialized construction, and particularly the attempt to create an anonymous architecture for mass society and a technological aesthetic for the machine age, made a reconciliation between the two extremes of individual creativity and the general spirit of the people seem secondary. With their built architecture, the former Expressionists left to their imitators a repertoire of easily adaptable elements: pointed arches and triangular windows, parabolic portals, diamond-shaped or wicker-like ornament on facades, stepped or triangular gables, battered pillars and crenellated cornices. Much the same can be said of their drawing styles. Long after Expressionism's demise, competition entries and presentations continued to exhibit its overdrawn pathos and tempestuous rhetoric, though these were no longer justified by any comparable aesthetic or social vision.

Notes

1 Bruno Taut, *Die Stadtkrone*, Jena, 1919, p. 17.
2 "Deutsche Architekten", in: *Die Bauwelt*, vol. 10/23, 1919, p. 5 ff.
3 Paul Westheim, "Architektur", in: *Das Kunstblatt*, vol. 3/4, April 1919, p. 98.
4 Paul Westheim, loc. cit., p. 97 ff. – Walter Müller-Wulckow, "Vom Werden architektonischer Form", in: *Das Kunstblatt*, vol. 3/4, April 1919.
5 Paul Westheim, loc. cit., p. 98.
6 Walter Müller-Wulckow, loc. cit., p. 120.
7 Walter Müller-Wulckow, loc. cit., p. 122.
8 Adolf Behne, in: *Ausstellung für unbekannte Architekten*, Berlin 1919, no pagination.
9 Adolf Behne, loc. cit.
10 Hans Poelzig, "Festspielhaus in Salzburg", in: *Das Kunstblatt*, vol. 5/3, March 1921, p. 77.
11 (Walter Curt Behrendt), "Kunstausstellungen", in: *Kunst und Künstler*, vol. 18/4, January 1920, p. 184.
12 Bruno Taut, "Idealisten", in: *Freiheit*, March 28th, 1919.
13 Adolf Behne, "Bruno Taut", in: *Pan*, vol. 3/23, 1912-13, p. 538 ff. I have to thank Jürgen Scharfe for referring me to this essay. Therefore the use of the term 'expressionist architecture' can be dated earlier than I did in my book *Die Architektur des Expressionismus* (Stuttgart 1973, p. 9).
14 Reginald R. Isaacs, *Walter Gropius*, vol. 1, Berlin, 1983, p. 65.
15 Walter Curt Behrendt, *Der Kampf um den Stil*, Stuttgart, Berlin, 1920, p. 65.
16 Wenzel August Hablik, introduction to: *Schaffende Kräfte*, 1909.
17 Paul Scheerbart, "Rakkox der Billionär", quoted from: Paul Scheerbart, *Dichterische Hauptwerke*, Stuttgart, 1962, p. 236.
18 Hendrikus Theodorus Wijdeveld, "Wendingen", in: *Wendingen*, vol. 1/1, January 1918, p.1.
19 Hermann Obrist, *Neue Möglichkeiten in der bildenden Kunst. Essays*, Leipzig, 1903, p. 118. – Adolf Behne, *Die Wiederkehr der Kunst*, Leipzig, 1919, p. 86 ff.
20 Otto Bartning, *Vom neuen Kirchenbau*, Berlin 1919, p. 111.
21 Adolf Behne, *Die Wiederkehr der Kunst*, op. cit., p. 107.
22 Paul Wolf, *Städtebau. Das Formproblem der Stadt in der Vergangenheit und Zukunft*, Leipzig 1919, p. 3.
23 Karl Ernst Osthaus, *Grundzüge der Stadtentwicklung*, Hagen, 1918, p. 37.
24 Adolf Behne, "Wiedergeburt der Baukunst", in Bruno Taut, loc. cit., 1919, p. 116.
25 Hans Hansen, *Das Erlebnis der Architektur*, Cologne, 1920, p. 42.
26 Adolf Behne, *Die Wiederkehr der Kunst*, loc. cit., p. 13.
27 Theodor Däubler, "Bernhard Hoetger", in: *Der Cicerone*, vol. 13/22, 1921, p. 644.
28 Bruno Taut, *Die neue Baukunst in Europa und Amerika*, Berlin, 1929, p. 41.
29 Hermann Finsterlin to Erich Mendelsohn, March 22nd, 1924, Kunstbibliothek, Berlin.
30 Jan Frederik Staal, "Die Stadtkrone von Bruno Taut", in: *Wendingen*, vol. 2/4, 1919, p. 9 ff.
31 Here and in the following part see: Giovanni Fanelli, *Architettura Moderna in Hollanda 1900–1940*, Florence, 1968. – Wim de Wit, *De architectuur der Amsterdamse School*, catalogue Stedeldijk Museum, Amsterdam 1977. – Giovanni Fanelli, *Moderne architectuur in Nederland 1900–1940*, The Hague, 1978. – Wim de wit (ed.), *The Amsterdam School. Dutch Expressionist Architecture*, New York, Cambridge (Mass.), 1983.
32 Adolf Behne, "Holländische Baukunst in der Gegenwart", in: *Wasmuths Monatshefte für die Baukunst*, vol. 6/1–2, 1921–22, p. 6 – Hendrikus Theodorus Wijdeveld, "Het Park Meerwijk te Bergen", in: *Wendingen*, vol. 1/8, 1918, p. 5.
33 Otto Bartning, "Die Baukunst als Deuterin der Zeit", in: Otto Bartning, *Spannweite*, Bramsche 1958, p. 38.
34 Bruno Taut, loc. cit., 1929, p. 41.
35 Hendrikus Theodorus Wijdeveld, loc. cit., 1918, p. 1.

1 Wenzel August Hablik. Crystal Buildings. 1903.

17

2 Wenzel August Hablik. Crystal Buildings. c. 1903.

3 Wenzel August Hablik. The Deeper the Well you Descend, the Brighter Shine the Stars.
From a cycle of etchings completed 1909.

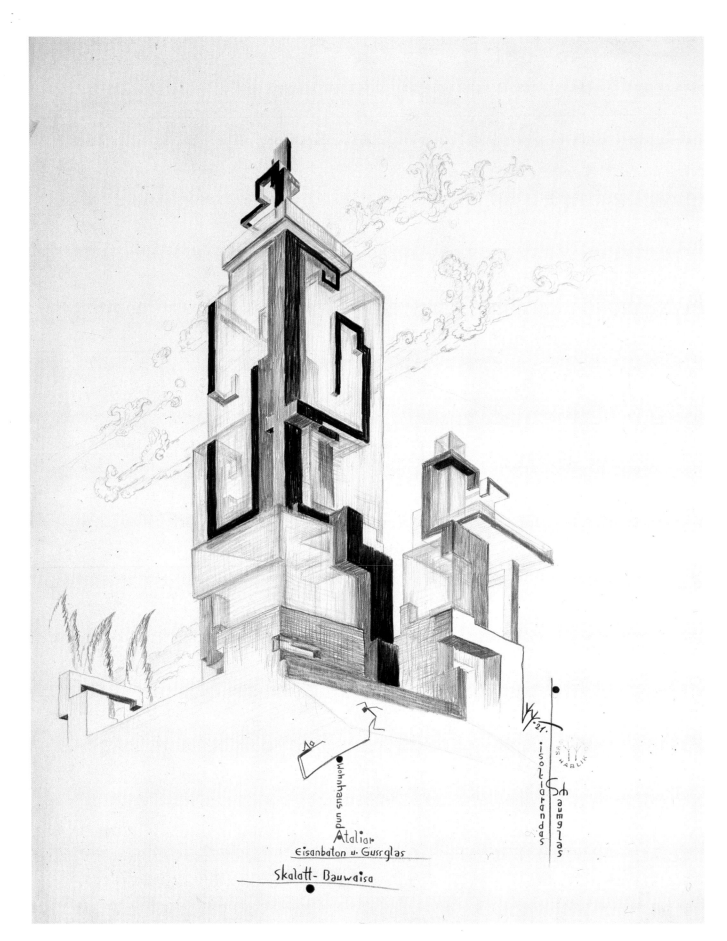

4 Wenzel August Hablik. Residence and Studio. 1921.

5 Wenzel August Hablik. Crystalline Chasm. c. 1920.

6 + 7 Wenzel August Hablik. *Top:* Canonical Buildings. *Bottom:* Explorers' Colony.
Both from a cycle of etchings completed 1925.

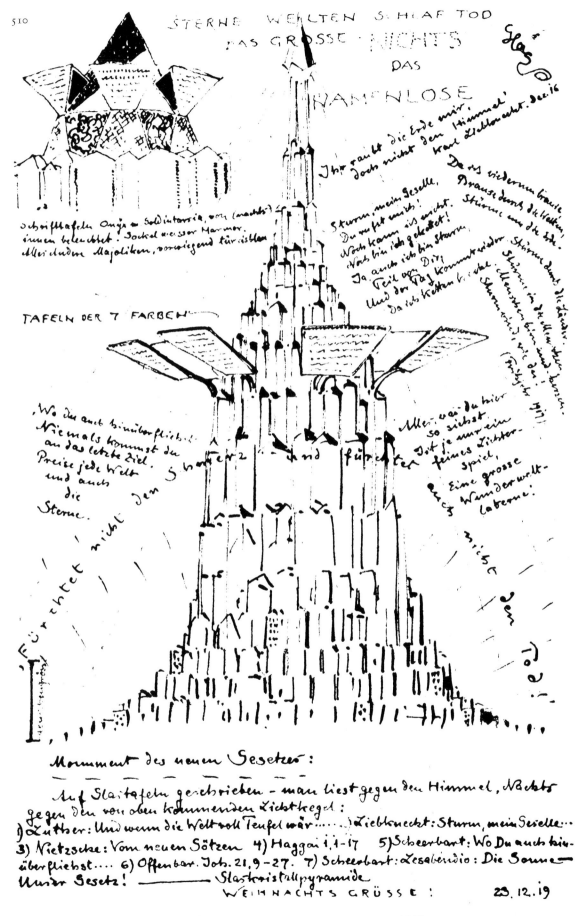

8 Bruno Taut. Monument of the New Law. 1919.

Der
Kristallberg

Der Fels ist
oberhalb der
Vegetations-
zone behauen
und geglättet
zu vielfachen
kristallinischen
Formen.

Die hinteren
Schneekuppen
sind mit
Glasbögen-
architektur
bebaut.

Vorne Kristall-
nadelpyra-
miden.

Über dem Ab-
grund eine
Brückenver-
gitterung aus
Glas.

9 Bruno Taut. The Crystal Mountain. 1918.

24

SCHNEE
GLETSCHER
GLAS

Firnen
im ewigen Eise
und Schnee —
überbaut und ge-
schmückt mit
Umbauungen, Flä-
chen und Blöcken
von farbigem Glase
— Bergblüten —

Die Ausführung ist gewiss ungeheuer schwer und opfervoll, aber nicht unmöglich . "Man verlangt so selten
von den Menschen das Unmögliche" (Goethe)

10 Bruno Taut. Snow Glacier Glass. 1918.

11 Bruno Taut. Untitled. 1919–20.

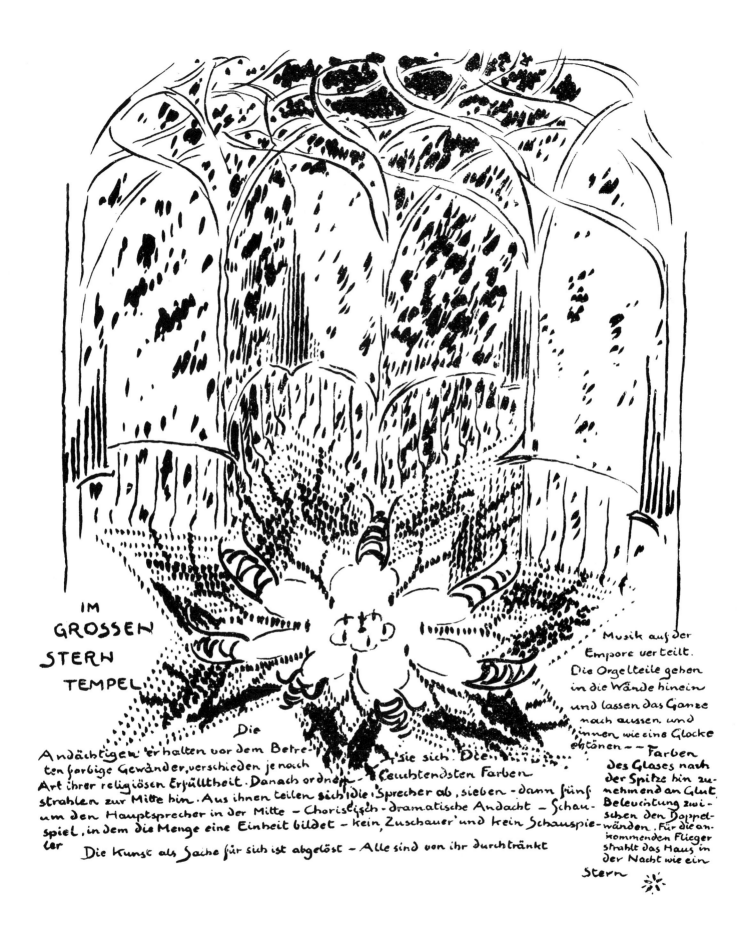

IM GROSSEN STERN TEMPEL

Die

Andächtigen erhalten vor dem Betreten farbige Gewänder, verschieden je nach Art ihrer religiösen Erfülltheit. Danach ordnen sie sich. Die leuchtendsten Farben strahlen zur Mitte hin. Aus ihnen teilen sich die Sprecher ab, sieben – dann fünf um den Hauptsprecher in der Mitte – Choristisch-dramatische Andacht – Schauspiel, in dem die Menge eine Einheit bildet – kein 'Zuschauer' und kein Schauspieler

Die Kunst als Sache für sich ist abgelöst – Alle sind von ihr durchtränkt

Musik aus der Empore verteilt. Die Orgelteile gehen in die Wände hinein und lassen das Ganze nach aussen und innen wie eine Glocke ertönen – – Farben des Glases nach der Spitze hin zunehmend an Glut Beleuchtung zwischen den Doppelwänden. Für die ankommenden Flieger strahlt das Haus in der Nacht wie ein Stern ✦

12 Bruno Taut. In the Great Temple of the Stars. 1919–20.

13 Max Taut. Untitled. 1919.

14 Max Taut. Blossom House. 1921.

15 Max Taut. House of the People. 1922.

16 Jefim Golyscheff. Untitled. c. 1919.

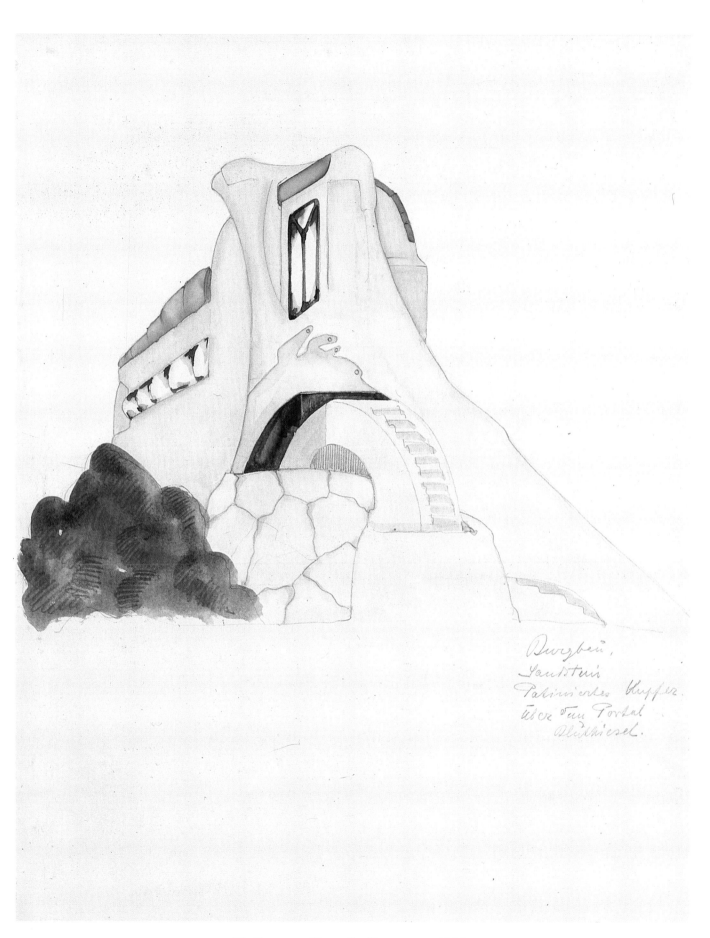

17 Hermann Finsterlin. Fortress. c. 1920.

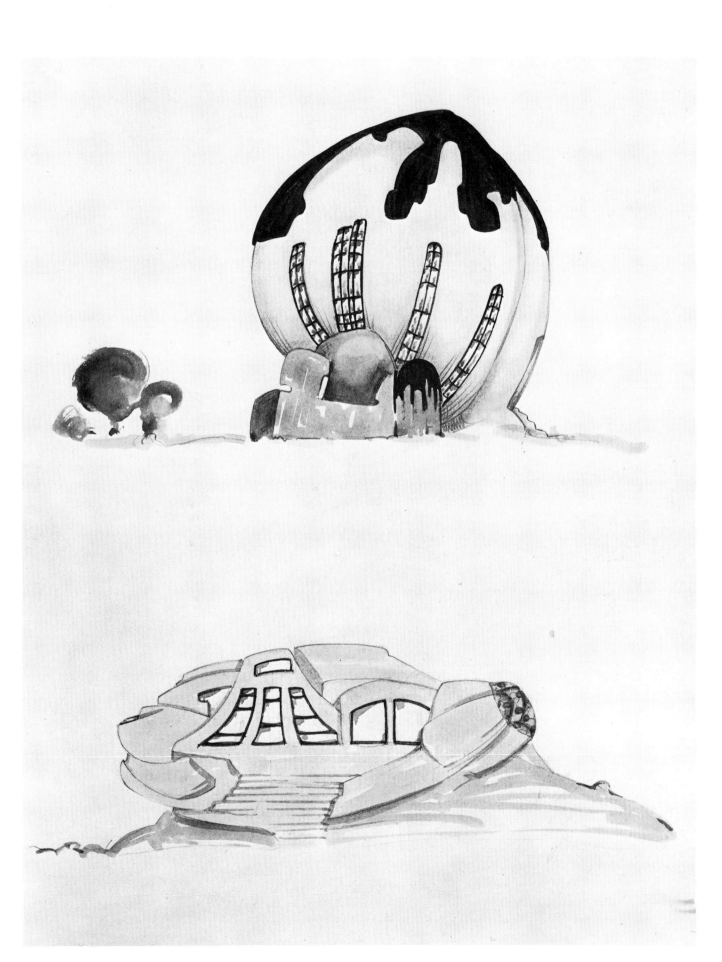

18 Hermann Finsterlin. House of Worship, Museum. 1915 (?).

19 + 20 Hermann Finsterlin. *Top:* Assembly Room. c. 1920. *Bottom:* Dream in Glass. 1920.

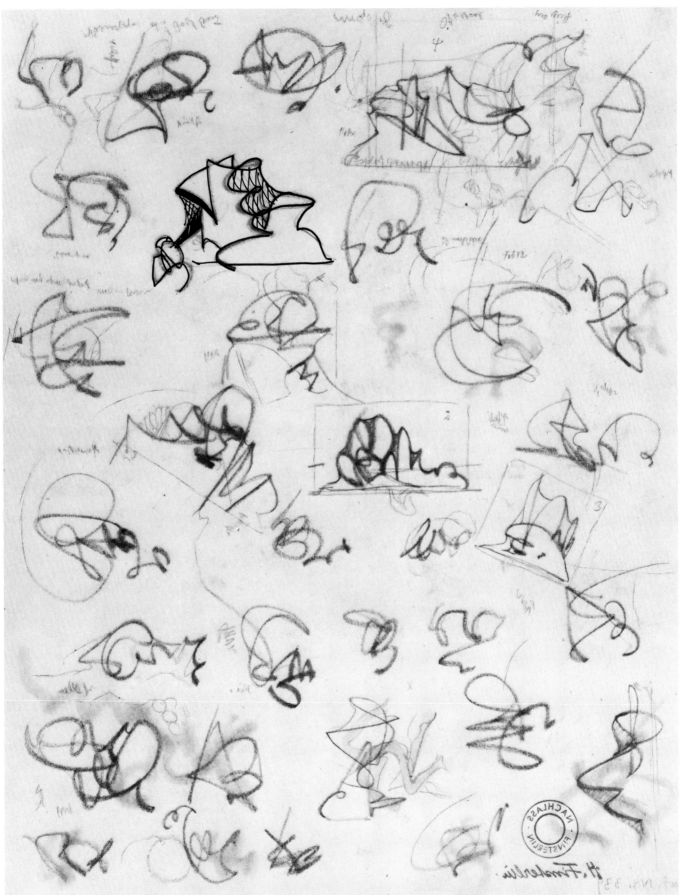

21 Hermann Finsterlin. Sketchbook page. c. 1920 and later.

22 Carl Krayl. Untitled. c. 1920.

23 Carl Krayl. Untitled. c. 1920.

24 Wassili Luckhardt. Crystal on Sphere. c. 1920.

25 Wassili Luckhardt. Monument to Labour. 1919.

26 Hans Luckhardt. Fantasy in Form. 1920 or earlier.

27 Paul Goesch. City Hall. c. 1920.

28 Paul Goesch. Temple. c. 1919.

29 Hans Scharoun. Bismarck Tower. c. 1910–11.

30 Hans Scharoun. Untitled. c. 1919.

31 Hans Scharoun. Gate and Door. c. 1919.

32 Hans Scharoun. Untitled. c. 1919.

33 Hans Scharoun. Theatre. c. 1922.

34 Hans Scharoun. Cinema II. c. 1922.

35 Hans Scharoun. Principles of Architecture. c. 1919.

36 Hans Scharoun. Sky, Waves, Wings. c. 1919.

37 Hugo Häring. Sketches of Apartment Buildings. 1921.

38 Hugo Häring. High-rise Building at Friedrichstrasse Station, Berlin. 1922.

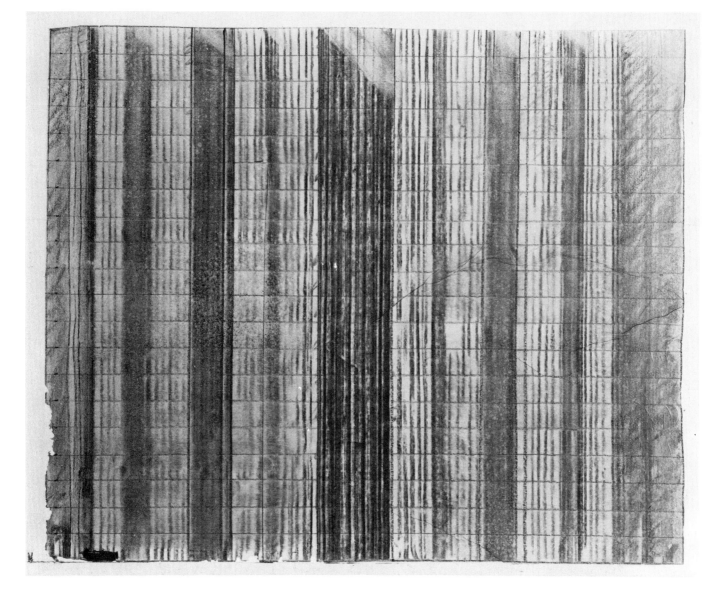

39 Ludwig Mies van der Rohe. High-rise Building at Friedrichstrasse Station, Berlin. 1921.

40 Ludwig Mies van der Rohe. High-rise Building at Friedrichstrasse Station, Berlin. 1921.

41 Friedrich Hugo Kaldenbach. Large Country Residence. 1914.

42 Johannes Molzahn. Untitled. 1918.

55

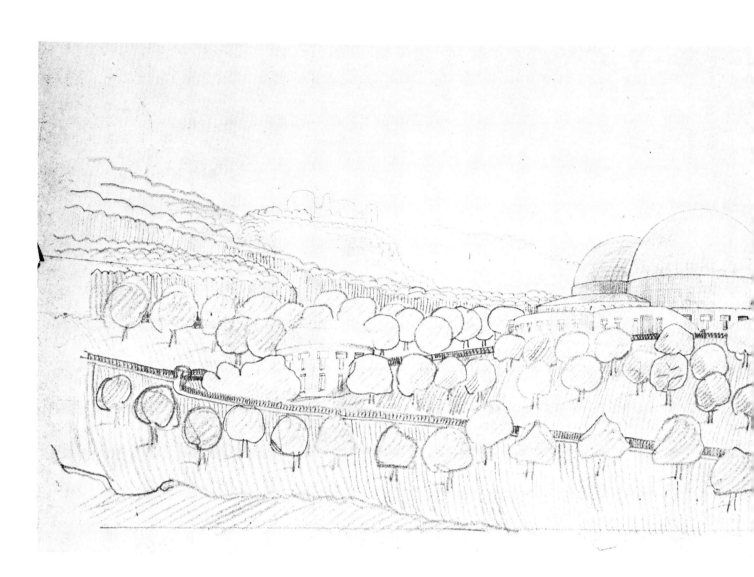

43 Rudolf Steiner (draughtsman unknown, possibly Carl Schmid-Curtius). Study for First Goetheanum. c. 1913.

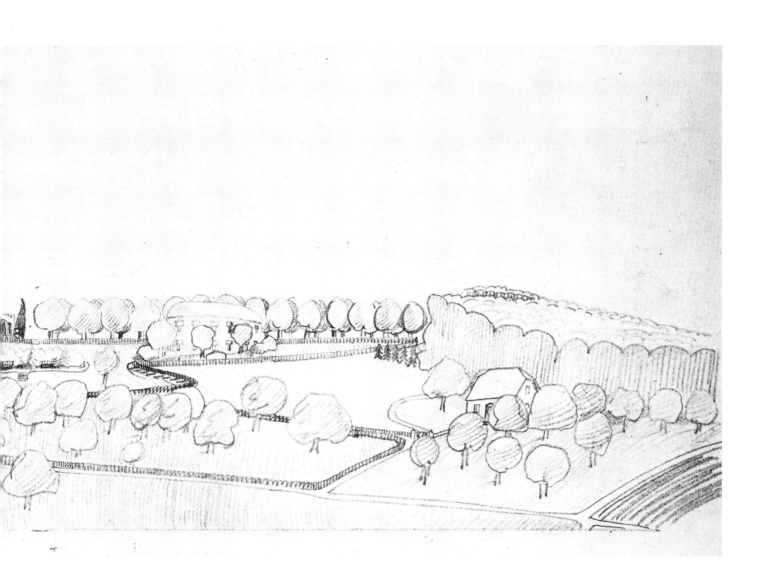

7. Jan. 1924. Vorm.

44 Rudolf Steiner. Motif for Second Goetheanum. 1924.

45 + 46 Walter Gropius and Adolf Meyer (draughtsman unknown). Kallenbach Residence, Berlin. 1921.

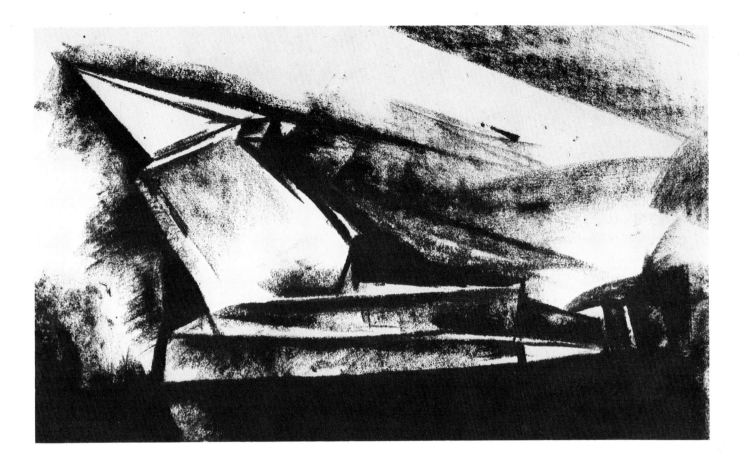

47 Walter Gropius (draughtsman unknown, possibly Farkas Molnár). Monument to the March Dead, Weimar. 1920–21.

48 Uriel Birnbaum. Bridge City. 1921–22.

49 Uriel Birnbaum. Kaleidoscope City. 1921–22.

61

50 Paul Thiersch. Central Building in a Large City. c. 1920.

51 Paul Thiersch. Academy of Philosophy, Erlangen. 1924.

52 Paul Thiersch. Central Building in a Large City. c. 1924.

53 Erich Mendelsohn. Becker Residence, Chemnitz. 1915.

54 Erich Mendelsohn. Becker Residence, Chemnitz. 1915.

55 + 56 Erich Mendelsohn. *Top:* Observatory. 1917. *Bottom:* Untitled. 1917.

57 Erich Mendelsohn. Small Dancing School. 1917.

58 Erich Mendelsohn. Film Studio. c. 1918. 59 Erich Mendelsohn. Warehouse. 1918.

60 Erich Mendelsohn. Tower in a Garden City, Haifa. 1923.

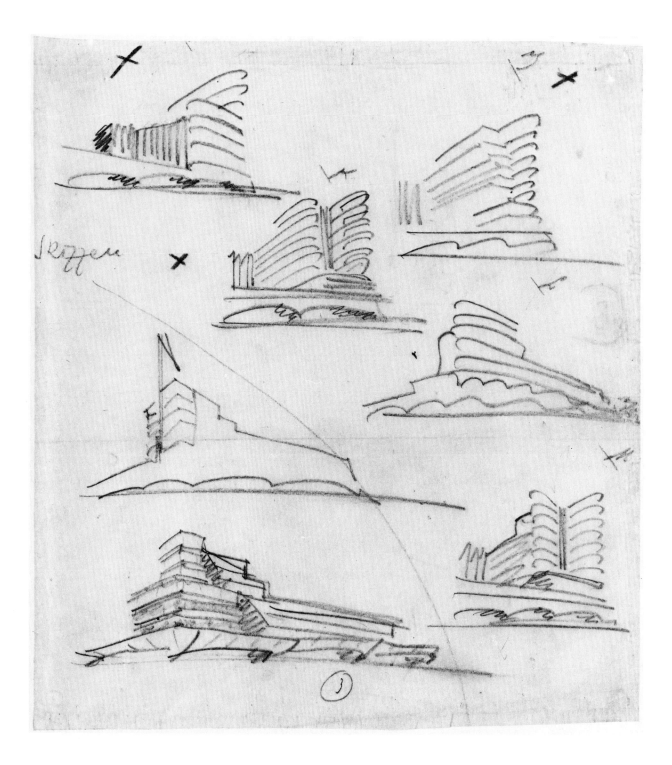

61 Erich Mendelsohn. High-rise Building on Kemperplatz, Berlin. 1922.

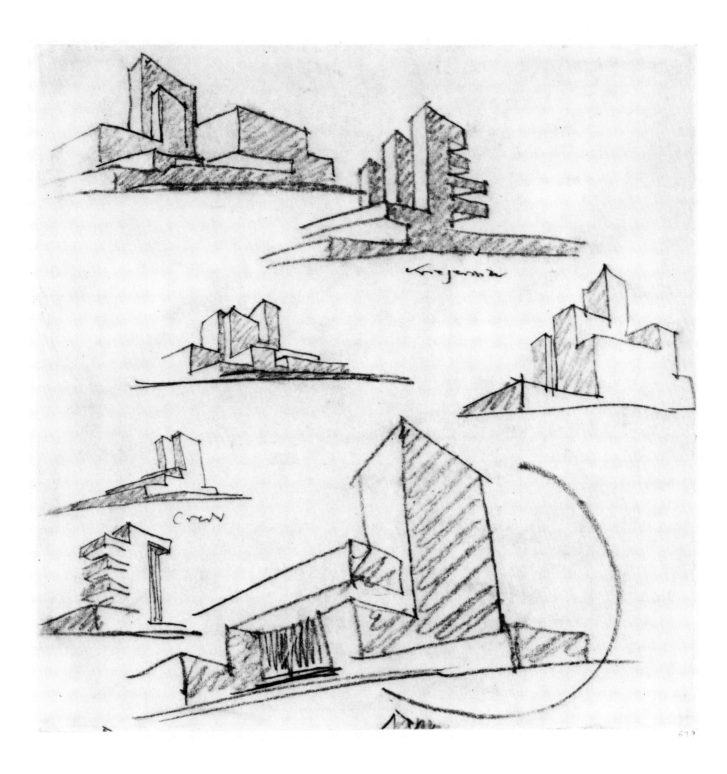

62 Erich Mendelsohn. Belligerent Credo. 1923.

63 Hans Poelzig. Columns. c. 1919.

64 Hans Poelzig. Theatre. c. 1920.

65 Hans Poelzig. Untitled. c. 1920.

66 Hans Poelzig. Sketchbook page: Order, Un-Ordered Cloud Forms. c. 1920.

67 Hans Poelzig. Untitled. c. 1920.

68 Hans Poelzig. Untitled. Date unknown.

69 Hans Poelzig. Sketchbook page. c. 1920 or later.

70 Fritz Höger. Design Sketches for the Chile Building, Hamburg. c. 1922.

71 Peter Behrens (draughtsman unknown). Main Hall, Hoechst Pigment and Dye Corporation. c. 1920.

72 Peter Behrens (draughtsman unknown). Colour sketch for the Main Hall,
Hoechst Pigment and Dye Corporation. c. 1920.

73 Erich Kettelhut. Metropolis, Second Version. The New Tower of Babel. 1925.

74 Erich Kettelhut. Metropolis, Second Version. Dawn. 1925.

75 Otto Bartning. Schuster Residence, Wylerberg bei Kleve. 1921.

76 Otto Bartning. Church, Constance. 1923.

77 Dominikus Böhm. Church Interior. c. 1925.

78 Dominikus Böhm. Soldiers' Memorial Church, Göttingen. c. 1923.

79 Rudolf Schwarz. Gloria. c. 1920.

80 Rudolf Schwarz. Untitled. c. 1920.

81 Hendrik Petrus Berlage. Pantheon of Humanity. 1915.

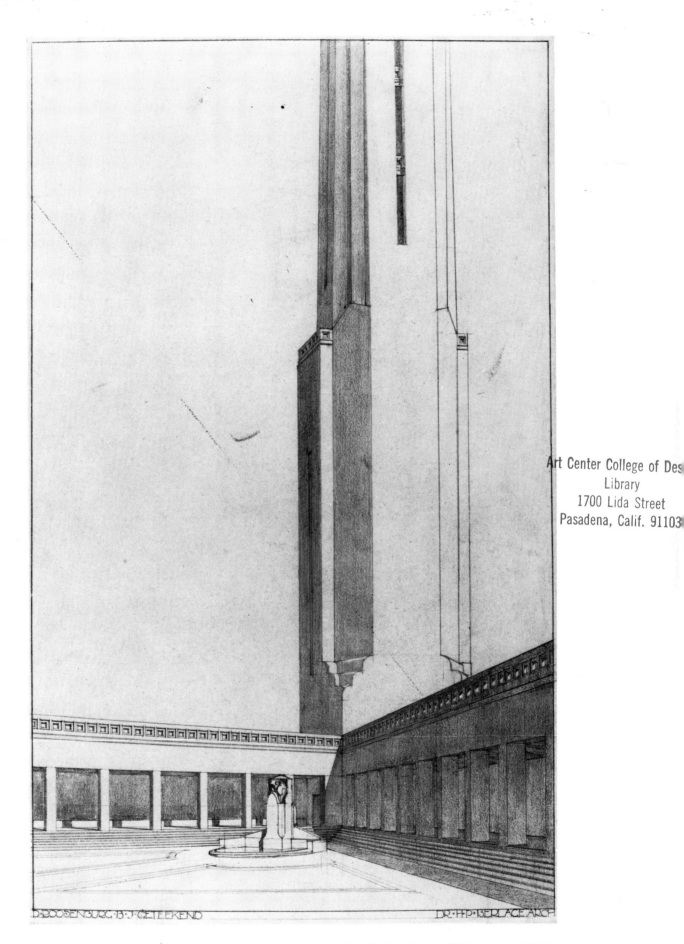

82 Hendrik Petrus Berlage (draughtsman: D. Roosenburg). Pantheon of Humanity. 1915.

83 Hendrik Petrus Berlage (in cooperation with E. E. Strasser and B. Wille). Lenin Mausoleum, Moscow. 1926.

84 Hendrik Petrus Berlage (in cooperation with E. E. Strasser and B. Wille). Lenin Mausoleum, Moscow. 1926.

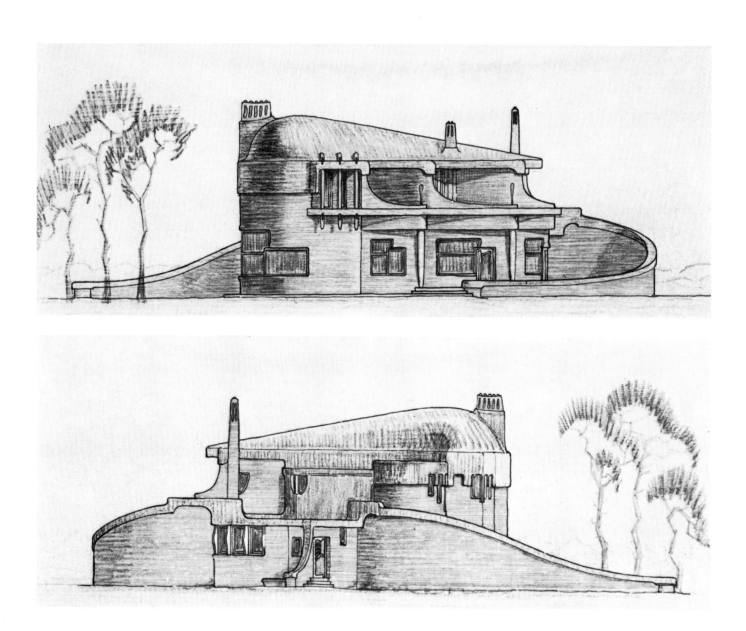

85 + 86 Adolf Eibink and J. A. Snellebrand. Small Country House in the Dunes.
Top: North elevation. *Bottom:* South elevation. 1917.

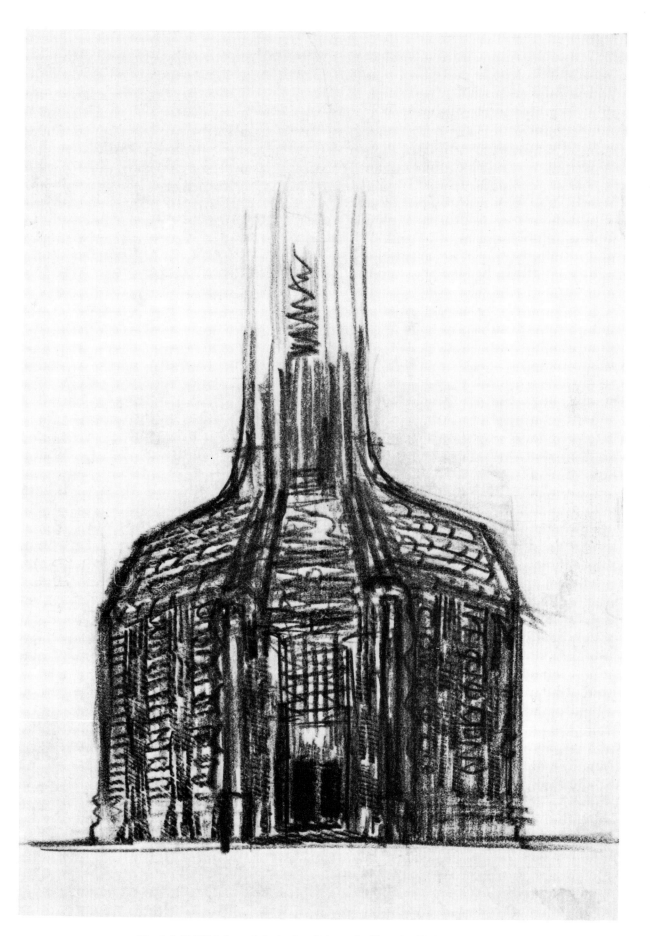

87 Adolf Eibink and J. A. Snellebrand. Church, Elshout. 1916.

88 Johannes Christiaan van Epen. Architectural Fantasy. c. 1920.

89 Johannes Christiaan van Epen. Skyscraper. c. 1920.

90 Michel de Klerk. Architectural Study. 1915.

91 Michel de Klerk. Van Leening Bank Building, Amsterdam. 1915.

92 + 93 Michel de Klerk. Apartment Block 2, Spaarndammerplantsoen, Amsterdam.
Top: perspective view. *Bottom:* exterior ornament. c. 1914–16.

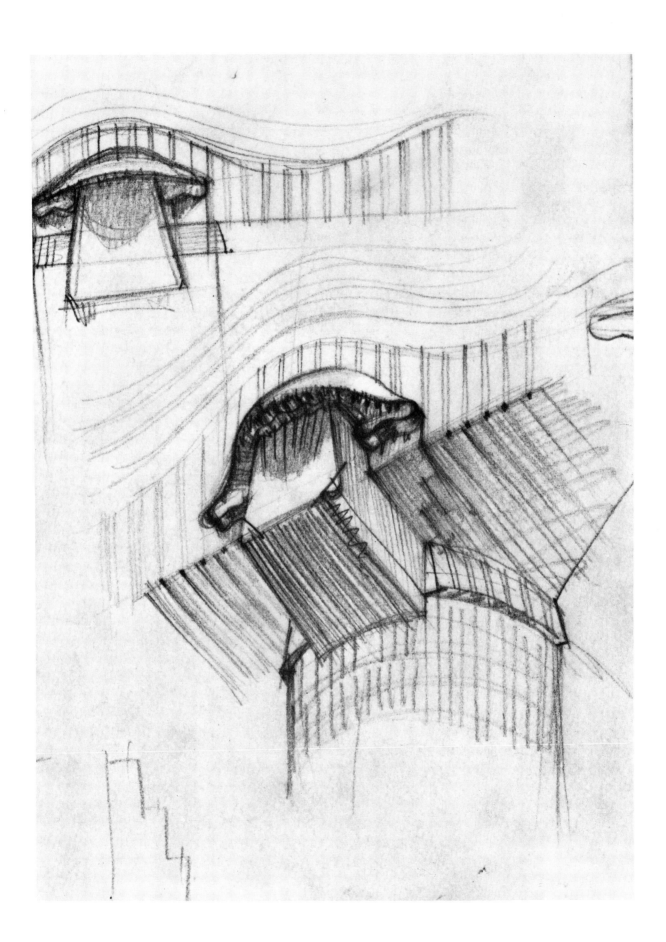

94 Michel de Klerk. Apartment Block 2, Spaarndammerplantsoen, Amsterdam. Detail of entrance. c. 1914–16.

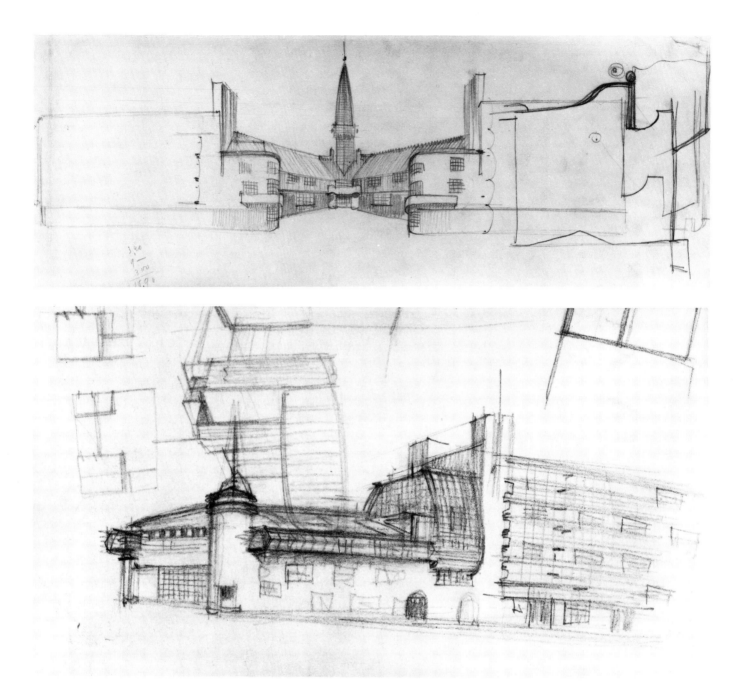

95, 96, 97 Michel de Klerk. Apartment Block 3, Spaarndammerplantsoen, Amsterdam. c. 1917–20.
Above: perspectives. *Right:* chimney.

103

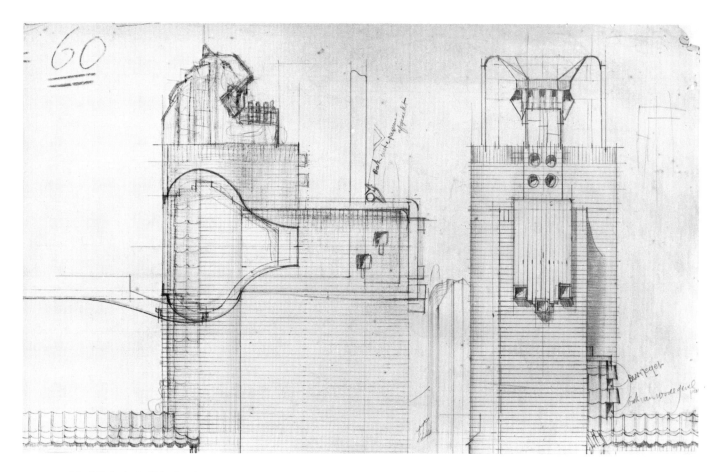

98 Michel de Klerk. Apartment Block 3, Spaarndammerplantsoen, Amsterdam. Chimney. c. 1917–20.

99 Michel de Klerk. Auction Hall for Flower Sales, Aalsmeer. 1923.

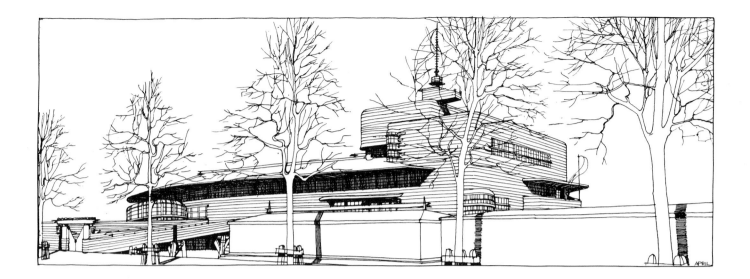

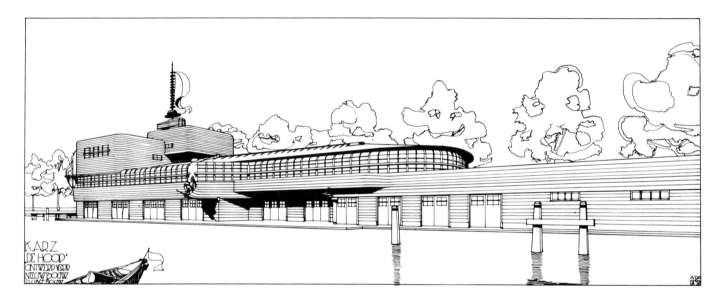

100 + 101 Michel de Klerk. De Hoop Boat Club, Amsterdam. 1922.

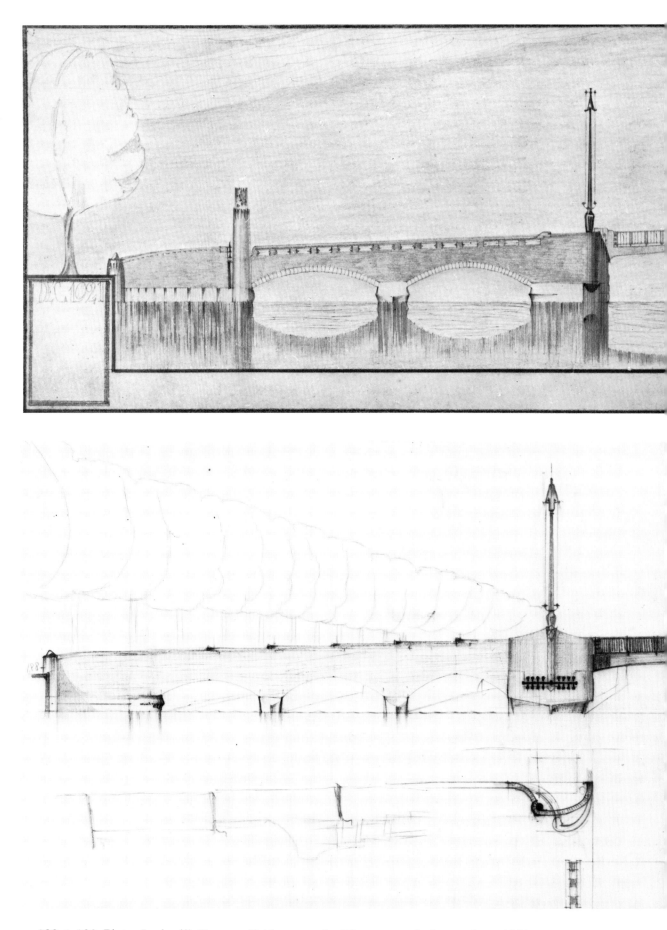

102 + 103 Pieter Lodewijk Kramer. Bridge over the Binnenamstel, Amsterdam. 1921.

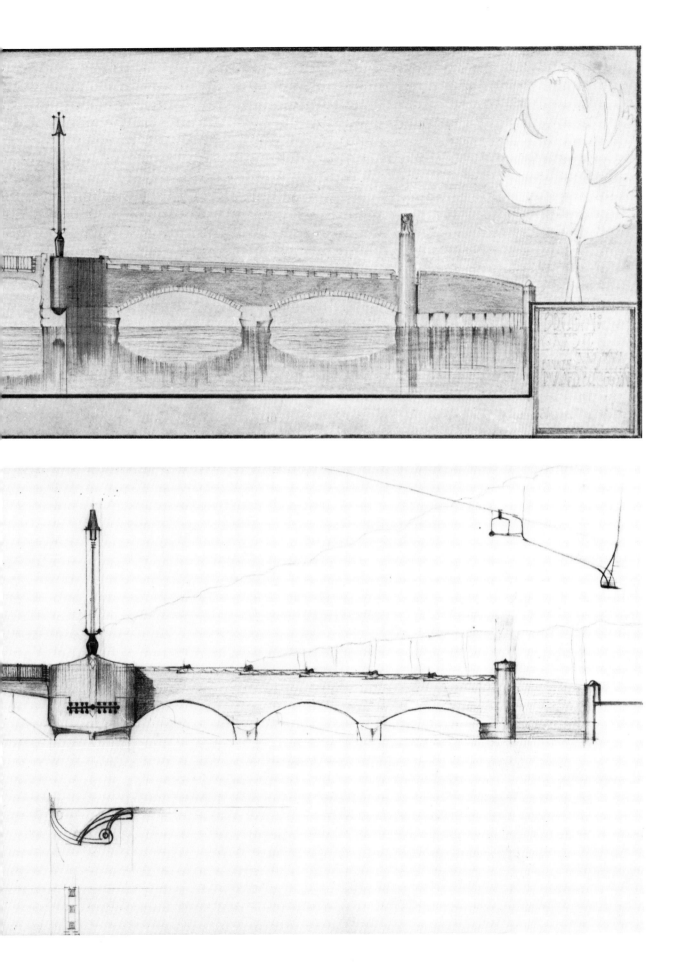

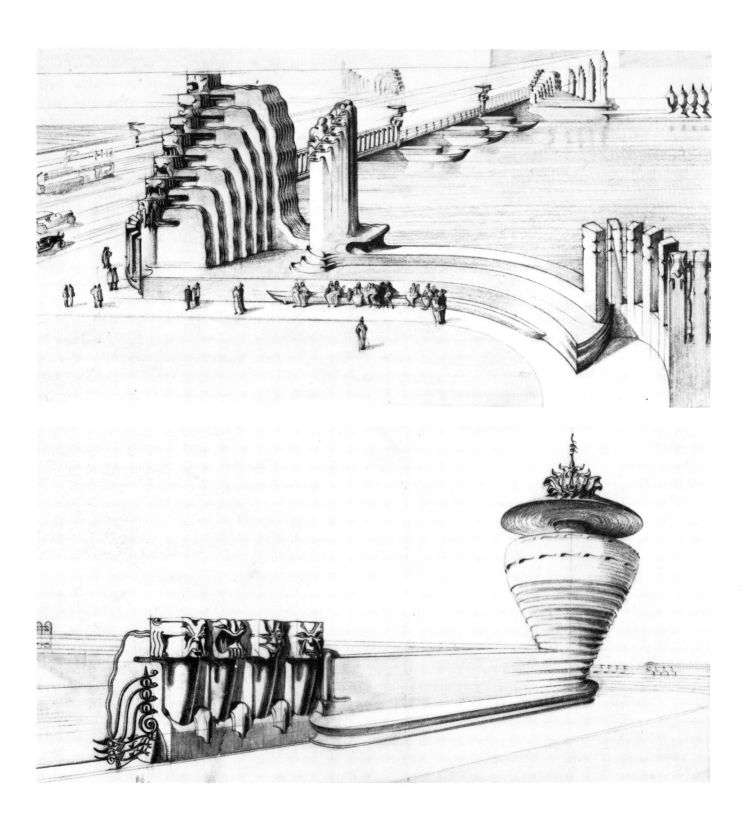

104 + 105 Hendrikus Theodorus Wijdeveld. Bridge on the Leidseplein, Amsterdam. c. 1920.

106 Hendrikus Theodorus Wijdeveld. Large Popular Theatre, Vondelpark, Amsterdam. c. 1919.

107 Willem Kromhout. Heineken's Brewery, Rotterdam. First design. 1925.

List of Plates

Wenzel August Hablik
b. 1881 Brüx, Bohemia – d. 1934 Itzehoe. Became a master cabinetmaker
in 1895; studied applied art and painting
from 1897 to 1906 at Teplitz Trade
School, the Vienna School of Arts and
Crafts, and the Prague Academy of
Arts. Lived in Itzehoe from 1907 on.
Member of Arbeitsrat für Kunst, correspondent of Die Gläserne Kette.

1 Crystal Buildings. 1903. Watercolour
and graphite. Signed and dated. 20
x 15.2 cm. Susanne Klingeberg, Hablik
Collection, Itzehoe.
2 Crystal Buildings. c. 1903. Coloured
pencil. Not signed or dated. 29.8 x
31.4 cm. Susanne Klingeberg, Hablik
Collection, Itzehoe.
3 The Deeper the Well You Descend,
the Brighter Shine the Stars. From the
cycle *Schaffende Kräfte* (Creative
Forces). 1909. Etching. 18.8 x 18.8 cm.
4 Residence and Studio. 1921. Coloured
pencil, graphite. Inscribed: *Residence
and Studio, reinforced concrete and
glass blocks, skeleton method of construction, insulating foamed glass.* Signed
and dated. 61.5 x 50 cm. Susanne Klingeberg, Hablik Collection, Itzehoe.
5 Crystalline Chasm. c. 1920. Graphite.
Not signed or dated. 32.6 x 24.8 cm.
Susanne Klingeberg, Hablik Collection,
Itzehoe.
6 Canonical Buildings. From the cycle
Cyklus Architektur – Übergangsbauten
(Architectural Cycle – Buildings for
the Interim). Completed 1925. Etching.
Inscribed: *Canonical buildings, reinforced concrete, moulded, calcite, crystal.*
20 x 16 cm, trapezoidal format. Susanne
Klingeberg, Hablik Collection, Itzehoe.
7 Explorers' Colony. From the cycle
Cyklus Architektur – Übergangsbauten
(Archtectural Cycle – Buildings for
the Interim). Completed 1925. Etching.
Inscribed: *Suspended metal sphere, light
as aluminium, hard as steel, transparent
as glass. Explorers' colony.* 20 x 16 cm,
trapezoidal format. Susanne Klingeberg,
Hablik Collection, Itzehoe.

Bruno Taut
b. 1880 Königsberg – d. 1938 Istanbul.
Studied 1900–01 and 1908–09 at the
Königsberg School of Building Trades
and at Berlin-Charlottenburg Technical
College. Chairman of the architectural
committee, Arbeitsrat für Kunst, and
founder of Die Gläserne Kette. City
Architect of Magdeburg from 1921–24.
Professor of Housing at Berlin Technical
College, 1930–32. Emigrated to Japan
in 1933, then in 1936 to Turkey.

8 Monument of the New Law. From
the correspondence of Die Gläserne
Kette. 23 December 1919. Photostat.

Signed ("Glas") and dated. 34.5 x
22 cm. The text reads:
*Stars Worlds Sleep Death
The great NOTHING the NAMELESS
Glass
Inscribed tablets onyx, gold intarsias,
lit from (night-time) within. Plinth white
marble. All the rest majolica, mostly
turquoise blue.
You steal the Earth from me, / But not
the Sky! / Karl Liebknecht, Dec. [19]16
Storm, my companion, / You call me! /
I cannot yet – / I am still in chains! /
I too am a Storm, / A part of you, /
And the day will come again / When
I will break the chains, / When I will
surge again, / Surge through the worlds, /
Storm round the Earth, / Storm through
the lands, / Storm into Man, / Human
brain and heart, / Storm wind, like
you! / Spring 1919.
Tablets of the 7 colours. / Wherever
you may seek refuge, / You will never
come to the ulitmate goal. / Praise every
World and also the Stars. / Fear not
pain and fear not death! / All that you
see here / Is only a cunning play of
lights, / A great Cosmic Magic Lantern!
Monument of the new Law: / Written
on tablets of glass – and read against
the sky, or at night against the beams
of light from above: / 1) Luther: And
if the world were full of devils ... 2)
Liebknecht: Storm, my companion ...
3) Nietzsche: Of the new idol ... 4) Hag-
gai 1, 1–17 5) Scheerbart: Wherever
you may seek refuge ... 6) Revelation
of St. John the Divine, chap. 21, 9–27.
7) Scheerbart: Lesabendio: The Sun –
Our Law! – Glass Crystal Pyramid /
CHRISTMAS GREETINGS!
23. 12. 1919.*
9 The Crystal Mountain (*Alpine Architektur.* Hagen, 1919. Sheet 7). Original drawing 1918. Watercolour and
india ink. Inscribed: *The crystal mountain. Above the vegetation the rock is
rough-hewn and smoothed into many
crystalline shapes. The snowy summits
in the background are crowned by glass-
arch architecture. In the foreground
pyramids of crystal needles. Over the
ravine a trellis-like glass bridge.* Not
signed or dated. 49.5 x 50 cm. Private
Collection, Berlin.
10 Snow Glacier Glass (*Alpine Architektur.* Hagen, 1919. Sheet 10). Original drawing 1918. Watercolour and
india ink. Inscribed: *Snow glacier glass.
Snowfields in the eternal ice and snow –
built up and decorated by superstructures.
Surface and blocks of coloured glass.
Mountain blossoms. The execution is
certainly very difficult but not impossible.
'Very rarely is the impossible asked
of men' (Goethe).* Not signed or dated.
46 x 41.5 cm. Private Collection, Berlin.
11 Untitled. From *Die Auflösung der
Städte* (Dispersing the Cities). Hagen,
1920. Plate 11. 1919–20.

12 In the Great Temple of the Stars.
From *Die Auflösung der Städte* (Dispersing the Cities). Hagen, 1920. Plate 18.
1919–20. Inscribed: *In the great temple
of the stars. The devout receive coloured
garments before entering, differing according to their religious convictions.
After that they arrange themselves in
order. The most luminous colours shine
towards the centre. The speakers divide
themselves from them, seven, then five
round the chief speaker in the centre.
Choral dramatic devotion. Performance,
in which the mass forms a unity – no
spectator and no actor. Art as a thing
in itself has disappeared – all men are
impregnated with it. Music is distributed
from the gallery. The organ-parts go
inside the walls and make the whole
outside and inside resound like a bell.
The colours of the glass increase in inten-
sity towards the top. Illumination between
the double walls. The house shines like
a star at night for the arriving aviators.*

Max Taut
b. 1884 Königsberg – d. 1967 Berlin.
Trained in carpentry and at the Königsberg School of Building Trades. Member
of Arbeitsrat für Kunst, correspondent
of Die Gläserne Kette. Head of Architecture Department, Berlin College
of Visual Arts, 1945–54.

13 Untitled. 1919. Graphite. Signed
and dated. 15.5 x 9.6 cm. Private collection, Berlin.
14 Blossom House. 1921. Watercolour,
india ink and graphite. Signed and
dated. 35.5 x 22 cm. Private collection,
Berlin.
15 House of the People. 1922. Watercolour, graphite and charcoal. Signed
and dated. 19.5 x 25.5 cm. Private collection, Berlin.

Jefim Golyscheff
b. 1897 Kherson, Ukraine – d. 1970
Paris. Trained as a concert violinist.
Studied painting at the Odessa Academy
of Art. Lived from 1909 to 1933 in
Berlin, working as a composer, musician,
painter and graphic artist. Participated
in the "Exhibition for Unknown Architects", Berlin, 1919. Emigrated in
1933; lived in Spain, France, Germany
and Brazil.

16 Untitled. c. 1919. India ink. Signed,
not dated. 13.5 x 15 cm. Private collection, Berlin.

Hermann Finsterlin
b. 1887 Munich – d. 1973 Stuttgart.
Studied natural sciences at Munich University and, in 1913, painting at Munich
Art Academy. Member of Arbeitsrat
für Kunst, correspondent of Die
Gläserne Kette. Lived in Stuttgart from
1926 on.

17 Fortress. c. 1920. Watercolour and graphite. Inscribed: *castle building, sandstone, patinated copper pebbles over the gate.* Not signed (signed on cardstock mount), not dated. 36.7 x 28 cm. Staatsgalerie Stuttgart.
18 House of Worship, Museum. 1915(?). Watercolour and graphite. Not signed (signed on cardstock mount), not dated (dated on mount: 1915). 37.8 x 28 cm. Staatsgalerie Stuttgart.
19 Assembly Room. c. 1920. Watercolour and graphite. Signed, not dated. 24.1 x 34.8 cm. Ungers Collection, Cologne.
20 Dream in Glass. 1920. Watercolour, graphite and india ink. Signed and dated. 19 x 29 cm. Staatsgalerie Stuttgart.
21 Sketchbook page. c. 1920 and later. Graphite, red pencil and ballpoint pen on tracing paper. Signed, not dated. Siegfried Cremer Collection, Landesmuseum für Kunst und Kulturgeschichte, Münster.

Carl Krayl
b. 1890 Weinsberg, Württemberg – d. 1947 Werder, Havel. Attended the Stuttgart School of Applied Art and Stuttgart Technical College, 1910–12. Member of Arbeitsrat für Kunst and correspondent of Die Gläserne Kette. Lived in Magdeburg from 1921–38.

22 Untitled. c. 1920. Graphite. Not signed or dated. 32.8 (16.4 folded) x 21 cm. Ungers Collection, Cologne.
23 Untitled. c. 1920. Graphite. Signed in another hand, not dated. 25.7 x 31.8 cm. Ungers Collection, Cologne.

Wassili Luckhardt
b. 1889 Berlin – d. 1972 Berlin. Attended Berlin and Dresden Technical Colleges. Member of Arbeitsrat für Kunst, correspondent of Die Gläserne Kette. Entered partnership with his brother Hans in 1921, and collaborated from 1924–37 with Alfons Anker.

24 Crystal on Sphere. c. 1920. Gouache. Not signed or dated. 47 x 97 cm Akademie der Künste, Berlin.
25 Monument to Labour. *"An die Freude"* (To Joy). 1919. Gouache on cardstock. Not signed or dated. 74 x 130 cm. Akademie der Künste, Berlin.

Hans Luckhardt
b. 1890 Berlin – d. 1954 Bad Wiessee, Upper Bavaria. Studied at Karlsruhe Technical College. Member of Arbeitsrat für Kunst, correspondent of Die Gläserne Kette. Entered partnership with his brother Wassili in 1921, and collaborated from 1924–37 with Alfons Anker.

26 Fantasy in Form. 1920 or earlier. From *Ruf zum Bauen* (A Call to Build),

second book publication of the Arbeitsrat für Kunst, Berlin, 1920.

Paul Goesch
b. 1885 Schwerin – d. 1940 Hartheim an der Donau. Attended Berlin-Charlottenburg Technical College from 1903. Government Architect. Member of Arbeitsrat für Kunst, correspondent of Die Gläserne Kette. Internment in psychiatric hospitals. Executed by the National Socialists.

27 City Hall. c. 1920. Watercolour and india ink. Not signed or dated. 16.2 x 20.8 cm. Ungers Collection, Cologne.
28 Temple. c. 1919. Watercolour and india ink. Not signed or dated. 20.6 x 33 cm. Ungers Collection, Cologne.

Hans Scharoun
b. 1893 Bremen – d. 1972 Berlin. Attended Berlin-Charlottenburg Technical College, 1912–14. Member of Arbeitsrat für Kunst, correspondent of Die Gläserne Kette. Lived from 1919–25 in Insterburg, East Prussia. 1925–32 Professor at Breslau Academy of Fine and Applied Art. 1945–46 City Architect of Greater Berlin. 1946–58 Professor at Berlin Technical University.

29 Bismarck Tower. c. 1910–11. Graphite on cardstock. Not signed or dated. 23.7 x 31 cm. Akademie der Künste, Berlin.
30 Untitled. c. 1919. Watercolour and graphite. Not signed or dated. 47.6 x 36 cm. Akademie der Künste, Berlin.
31 Gate and Door. c. 1919. Watercolour and graphite. Not signed or dated. 49.8 x 35.4 cm. Akademie der Künste, Berlin.
32 Untitled. c. 1919. Watercolour and graphite. Not signed or dated. 49.8 x 35.4 cm. Akademie der Künste, Berlin.
33 Theatre. c. 1922. Watercolour and graphite. Not signed or dated. 31 x 22.9 cm. Akademie der Künste, Berlin.
34 Cinema II. c. 1922. Watercolour and graphite. Not signed or dated. 32.3 x 24.6 cm. Akademie der Künste, Berlin.
35 Principles of Architecture. c. 1919. Watercolour and graphite. Inscription illegible. Not signed or dated. 50.5 x 35.4 cm. Akademie der Künste, Berlin.
36 Sky, Waves, Wings. c. 1919. Watercolour and graphite. Inscription illegible. Not signed or dated. 35.4 x 25.1 cm. Akademie der Künste, Berlin.

Hugo Häring
b. 1882 Biberach – d. 1958 Göppingen. Attended Technical Colleges in Stuttgart, Berlin-Charlottenburg, and Dres-

den from 1899–1903. Headed former Reimann School, Berlin, from 1935–43. Moved to Biberach in 1943.

37 Sketches of Apartment Buildings. 1921. Graphite on tracing paper. Not signed or dated. Akademie der Künste, Berlin.
38 High-rise Building at Friedrichstrasse Station, Berlin. 1922. Charcoal. Inscription illegible. Signed and dated. Akademie der Künste, Berlin.

Ludwig Mies van der Rohe
b. 1886 Aachen – d. 1969 Chicago. Studied with Bruno Paul, 1905–07. Collaborated with Peter Behrens, 1908–11. 1930–33 Director of the Bauhaus, Dessau and Berlin. Emigrated to the U.S. in 1937. 1938–58 Chairman, Department of Architecture, Illinois Institute of Technology, Chicago.

39 High-rise Building at Friedrichstrasse Station, Berlin. 1921. Charcoal and graphite on tracing paper; motif cut out and mounted on paper. Not signed or dated. 55.2 x 87.6 cm. Museum of Modern Art, New York.
40 High-rise Building at Friedrichstrasse Station, Berlin. 1921. Charcoal and pencil. Not signed or dated. 173.5 x 122 cm. Museum of Modern Art, New York.

Friedrich Hugo Kaldenbach
b. 1887 Aachen-Burtscheid – d. 1918 Berlin. Studied at Düsseldorf School of Applied Art. 1911–14 Head of Arts and Crafts Seminar, Hagen. Collaborated with Walter Gropius and Adolf Meyer. Represented posthumously at Exhibition for Unknown Architects, Berlin, 1919.

41 Large Country Residence. 1914. Graphite. Signed and dated. 37.4 x 55.3 cm. Karl Ernst Osthaus Museum, Hagen.

Johannes Molzahn
b. 1892 Duisburg – d. 1965 Munich. Attended the Grand Duchy of Weimar Drawing School and took a course in photography. Participated in the Exhibition for Unknown Architects, Berlin, 1919. 1928–32 Professor, State Academy, Breslau. Emigrated in 1938 to the U.S. 1938–52 professorships and lecturership in Seattle, Chicago, and New York. Returned to Germany in 1959.

42 Untitled. 1918. Charcoal and graphite on tracing paper. Inscribed: *Entry: spiral suction form / Interior: Cascading coloured beams of light – space opening up more and more – ending in vault of great dome / Mural paintings: Cosmic composition / Dis-*

persed light filters: Tower-vault-dome / Coloured glass windows. Signed, not dated. 62.7 x 47 cm. Molzahn Bequest, Munich.

Rudolf Steiner
b. 1861 Kraljewic, Jugoslavia – d. 1925 Dornach bei Basel. Taught from 1898–1900 at Workingmens' College, Berlin. Became Head of the German Section, Theosophical Society, in 1902. Founded Anthroposophical Society in 1913.

43 Draughtsman unknown (Carl Schmid-Curtius?). Study for First Goetheanum, view from northwest. c. 1913. Photocopy (original graphite). Not signed or dated. 43 x 67.5 cm. Goetheanum, Freie Hochschule für Geisteswissenschaft, Dornach bei Basel.
44 Motif for Second Goetheanum. 1924. Coloured chalk on blackboard. Not signed, dated in another hand.

Walter Gropius
b. 1883 Berlin – d. 1969 Boston. Studied from 1903–07 at Technical Colleges, Munich and Berlin-Charlottenburg. Collaborated with Peter Behrens, 1907–10. Named Chairman, Arbeitsrat für Kunst, in 1919. 1919-28 Director of the Bauhaus, Weimar and Dessau. Emigrated to England in 1934, and in 1937 to the U.S. To 1952 Head, Department of Architecture, Harvard University, Cambridge, Mass.

Adolf Meyer
b. 1881 Mechernich, Eifel – d. 1929 near Baltrum, North Sea. Attended the Düsseldorf School of Applied Art from 1904–07. Collaborated with Peter Behrens from 1907–08. Partnership with Walter Gropius from 1911–25. Taught from 1919–25 at the Weimar Bauhaus, then joined Frankfurt City Building Administration.

45 Draughtsman unknown. Kallenbach Residence, Berlin. 1921. Charcoal. Not signed or dated. Busch-Reisinger Museum, Cambridge, Mass.
46 Draughtsman unknown. Kallenbach Residence, Berlin. 1921. Charcoal. Not signed or dated. Busch-Reisinger Museum, Cambridge, Mass.
Walter Gropius
For biographical data, see entries 45 and 46.
47 Draughtsman unknown (Farkas Molnar?). Monument to the March Dead, Weimar. 1920–21. Lithograph. Not signed or dated. 13.7 x 22 cm (sheet 29.9 x 46.6 cm). Bauhaus-Archiv, Berlin.

Uriel Birnbaum
b. 1894 Vienna – d. 1956 Amersfoort. Attended a Berlin art school for one

month in 1913. Seriously wounded in 1917. Wrote poetry, stories, short plays and essays; painted, drew and illustrated books. Emigrated in 1938 from Vienna to the Netherlands.

48 Bridge City. From *Der Kaiser und sein Architekt.* Leipzig and Vienna, 1924. Original drawing 1921–22. Coloured ink. Signed, not dated.
49 Kaleidoscope City. From *Der Kaiser und sein Architekt.* Leipzig and Vienna, 1924. Original drawing 1921–22. Coloured ink. Signed, not dated.

Paul Thiersch
b. 1879 Munich – d. 1928 Hanover. Studied from 1897–1905 at Technikum Winterthur, in the Department of Arts and Crafts at Basel Trade School, and at Munich Technical College. Collaborator of Peter Behrens and Bruno Paul. 1915–28 Director, Halle School of Applied Art. 1928 Professor, Hanover Technical College.

50 Central Building in a Large City. c. 1920. Graphite. Not signed or dated. 16 x 21.3 cm. Thiersch Archive, Überlingen.
51 Academy of Philosophy, Erlangen. 1924. Charcoal. Not signed or dated. 16.7 x 35 cm. Thiersch Archive, Überlingen.
52 Central Building in a Large City. c. 1924. Graphite. Not signed or dated. 25 x 20 cm. Thiersch Archive, Überlingen.

Erich Mendelsohn
b. 1887 Allenstein, East Prussia – d. 1953 San Francisco. Studied from 1908–12 at Berlin-Charlottenburg Technical College. Member of Arbeitsrat für Kunst. Emigrated to England in 1933 and to the U.S. in 1941.

53 Becker Residence, Chemnitz. 1915. Watercolour. Not signed or dated. 29.8 x 27.3 cm. Kunstbibliothek Berlin, Staatliche Museen Preussischer Kulturbesitz.
54 Becker Residence, Chemnitz. 1915. Watercolour on tracing paper. Not signed or dated. 29.1 x 27.4 cm. Kunstbibliothek Berlin, Staatliche Museen Preussischer Kulturbesitz.
55 Observatory. 1917. Graphite. Signed and dated. 12.1 x 12.1 cm Kunstbibliothek Berlin, Staatliche Museen Preussischer Kulturbesitz.
56 Untitled. 1917. India ink. Signed, dated. 9.5 x 9.5 cm. Kunstbibliothek Berlin, Staatliche Museen Preussischer Kulturbesitz.
57 Small Dancing School. 1917. Graphite. Not signed or dated. 14 x 12.6 cm. Kunstbibliothek Berlin, Staatliche Museen Preussischer Kulturbesitz.

58 Film Studio. c. 1918. From *Wendingen,* vol. 3, October 1920.
59 Warehouse. 1918. From *Wendingen,* vol. 3, October 1920.
60 Tower in a Garden City, Haifa. 1923. From *Erich Mendelsohn, Das Gesamtschaffen des Architekten. Skizzen, Entwürfe, Bauten.* Berlin, 1930.
61 High-rise Building on Kemperplatz, Berlin. 1922. Graphite and coloured pencil. Not signed or dated. 27.6 x 24.8 cm. Kunstbibliothek Berlin, Staatliche Museen Preussischer Kulturbesitz.
62 Belligerent Credo. 1923. Graphite on tracing paper. Not signed or dated. 21.6 x 20.9 cm. Kunstbibliothek Berlin, Staatliche Museen Preussischer Kulturbesitz.

Hans Poelzig
b. 1869 Berlin – d. 1936 Berlin. Attended Berlin-Charlottenburg Technical College from 1889–94. 1900 Lecturer and 1903–16 Director, College of Fine and Applied Art (Academy), Breslau. 1916–20 City Architect, Dresden. Member of Arbeitsrat für Kunst. 1924–35 Professor, Berlin Technical College.

63 Columns (executed in connection with the Grosses Schauspielhaus, Berlin). c. 1919. Coloured Chalk. Not signed or dated. 25.2 x 40.8 cm. Marlene Poelzig Collection, Plans Collection, University Library, Technische Universität Berlin.
64 Theatre (executed in connection with plans for a Festival Hall, Salzburg). c. 1920. Graphite. Not signed or dated. 19.3 x 27.2 cm. Marlene Poelzig Collection, Plans Collection, University Library, Technische Universität Berlin.
65 Untitled (perhaps executed in connection with plans for a Festival Hall, Salzburg). c. 1920. Chalk or charcoal on tracing paper. Not signed or dated. 19.6 x 27 cm. Marlene Poelzig Collection, Hamburg.
66 Order; Random Cloud Shapes (sketchbook page). c. 1920. Charcoal. Inscribed: *Order / Un-ordered cloud form / (?), see no longer little things / Correct the forms of the winds / Greatest cosmic feeling, / Affinity with Chinese world map, Cosmic feeling in the Rococo.* Not signed or dated. 32.8 x 25.6 cm. Marlene Poelzig Collection, Hamburg.
67 Untitled. c. 1920. Charcoal. Not signed or dated. 25.2 x 40.8 cm. Marlene Poelzig Collection, Plans Collection, University Library, Technische Universität Berlin.
68 Untitled. Chalk or charcoal. Not signed or dated. 25.4 x 32.8 cm. Marlene Poelzig Collection, Plans Collection,

University Library, Technische Universität Berlin.
69 Untitled (sketchbook page). c. 1920 or later. Graphite. Not signed or dated. 32.8 x 25.6 cm. Marlene Poelzig Collection, Hamburg.

Fritz Höger
b. 1877 Bekenreihe, Holstein – d. 1949 Bad Segeberg. Educated at the School for Building Trades, Hamburg, 1897–99. Became Professor for a short time in 1934 at the Northern College of Art, Bremen.

70 Design Sketches for the Chile Building, Hamburg. c. 1922. Graphite and pen and ink on tracing paper. Not signed or dated. 29.6 x 21 cm, sheet irregularly trimmed and damaged by fire. Kunstbibliothek Berlin, Staatliche Museen Preussischer Kulturbesitz.

Peter Behrens
b. 1868 Hamburg – d. 1940 Berlin. Studied painting from 1886–89 at Karlsruhe and Düsseldorf Academies. Named member of the Darmstadt Artists' Colony in 1900. 1903–07 Director, Düsseldorf College of Applied Art. Became artistic consultant to the AEG Company, Berlin, in 1907. 1922–36 Director, Advanced School of Architecture, Vienna Academy. Returned to Berlin thereafter.

71 Draughtsman unknown. Main Hall, Hoechst Pigment and Dye Corporation. c. 1920. Charcoal. Not signed or dated. 66 x 37 cm. Farbwerke Hoechst AG Archive.
72 Draughtsman unknown. Colour sketch for the Main Hall, Hoechst Pigment and Dye Corporation. c. 1920. From P. J. Cremers, *Peter Behrens*. Essen, 1928.

Erich Kettelhut
b. 1893 – d. 1979 Hamburg. Worked as a scene painter at the Berlin Municipal Opera, then began designing film sets in 1919. Collaborated with Otto Hunte and Karl Vollbrecht on the sets for Fritz Lang's film *Metropolis*.

73 Metropolis, Second Version. The New Tower of Babel. 1925. India ink and gouache. 45.5 x 55 cm. Stiftung Deutsche Kinemathek, Berlin.
74 Metropolis, Second Version. Dawn. 1925. India ink and gouache. 45.5 x 55 cm. Stiftung Deutsche Kinemathek, Berlin.

Otto Bartning
b. 1883 Karlsruhe – d. 1959 Darmstadt. Studied from 1904–08 at Berlin-Charlottenburg and Karlsruhe Technical Colleges. Member of Arbeitsrat für Kunst. 1926–30 Director, State College of

Architecture, Weimar. 1950–59 President, Association of German Architects.

75 Schuster Residence, Wylerberg bei Kleve. 1921. Graphite on tracing paper. Signed and dated. 54 x 72 cm. Otto Bartning Bequest, Technische Hochschule Darmstadt.
76 Church, Constance. 1923. Charcoal on tracing paper. Not signed or dated. 62 x 86 cm. Otto Bartning Bequest, Technische Hochschule Darmstadt.

Dominikus Böhm
b. 1880 Jettingen, Bavaria – d. 1955 Cologne. Studied at Augsburg School of Architecture and Stuttgart Technical College. 1908–26 Instructor and Professor, Offenbach School of Applied Art; 1926–34 and 1946–53, Cologne Schools of Applied Arts.

77 Church Interior (executed in connection with the Christkönigskirche, Mainz-Bischofsheim). c. 1925. Charcoal. Signed, not dated. 14.5 x 14 cm. Professor Gottfried Böhm, Cologne.
78 Soldiers' Memorial Church, Göttingen. c. 1923. Charcoal on yellow paper. Signed, not dated. 76 x 56 cm. Professor Gottfried Böhm, Cologne.

Rudolf Schwarz
b. 1897 Strassburg – d. 1961 Cologne. Studied at Berlin Technical College and the Prussian Academy of Arts, Berlin. 1927–34 Director, Aachen School of Applied Art. 1946–52 Head of Town Planning, City of Cologne. 1953–61 Professor, Düsseldorf Art Academy.

79 Gloria. c. 1920. Watercolour. Not signed or dated. 32.5 x 21.2 cm. Schwarz Archive, Cologne.
80 Untitled. c. 1920. Graphite on tracing paper. Not signed or dated. 26 x 28 cm, sheet irregularly trimmed. Schwarz Archive, Cologne.

Hendrik Petrus Berlage
b. 1856 Amsterdam – d. 1934 The Hague. Studied from 1875–78 at Zurich Technical College. Signed a five-year contract in 1913 with the architectural office of Wm. H. Müller & Co. Became Professor at Delft Technical College in 1924.

81 Pantheon of Humanity. 1915. Charcoal and graphite. Not signed or dated. 33 x 20 cm. Nederlands Documentatiecentrum voor de Bouwkunst, Amsterdam.
82 Draughtsman: D. Roosenburg. Pantheon of Humanity. 1915. Graphite. Signed, not dated. 41 x 26 cm. Nederlands Documentatiecentrum voor de Bouwkunst, Amsterdam.

83 (In cooperation with E. E. Strasser and B. Wille). Lenin Mausoleum, Moscow. 1926. Graphite on tracing paper. Not signed or dated. 92 x 77 cm. Nederlands Documentatiecentrum voor de Bouwkunst, Amsterdam.
84 (In cooperation with E. E. Strasser and B. Wille). Lenin Mausoleum, Moscow. 1926. Graphite on tracing paper. Not signed or dated. 92 x 77 cm. Nederlands Documentatiecentrum voor de Bouwkunst, Amsterdam.

Adolf Eibink
1893 – 1975

J. A. Snellebrand
1891 – 1963

85 Small Country House in the Dunes. North elevation. 1917. Coloured pencil. Not signed or dated. 16.5 x 37 cm. Nederlands Documentatiecentrum voor de Bouwkunst, Amsterdam.
86 Small Country House in the Dunes. South elevation. 1917. Coloured pencil. Not signed or dated. 16.5 x 37 cm. Nederlands Documentatiecentrum voor de Bouwkunst, Amsterdam.
87 Church, Elshout. Motto of the competition entry "Leo, het brandend hart der wereld". 1916. Charcoal on tracing paper. Not signed or dated. 28 x 19.5 cm. Nederlands Documentatiecentrum voor de Bouwkunst, Amsterdam.

Johannes Christiaan van Epen
b. 1880 Amsterdam – d. 1960. Trained with the Amsterdam architect A.C. Boerma, followed by three years of study in Paris.

88 Architectural Fantasy. c. 1920. Charcoal and wash on tracing paper. Not signed or dated. 41 x 22 cm. Nederlands Documentatiecentrum voor de Bouwkunst, Amsterdam.
89 Skyscraper. c. 1920. Charcoal on tracing paper. Signed (in another hand?), not dated. Inscription illegible. 40 x 28 cm, sheet trimmed irregularly. Nederlands Documentatiecentrum voor de Bouwkunst, Amsterdam.

Michel de Klerk
b. 1884 Amsterdam – d. 1923 Amsterdam. Worked in the office of Eduard Cuypers from 1898–1910. Collaborated from 1911–16 with Johan Melchior van der Mey and Piet Kramer on the Scheepvaarthuis, Amsterdam.

90 Architectural Study. Motto of the competition entry "Herfst". 1915. Graphite, coloured pencil and chalk. Not signed or dated. 47.6 x 28.1 cm. Nederlands Documentatiecentrum voor de Bouwkunst, Amsterdam.
91 Van Leening Bank Building, Amsterdam. 1915. Graphite and coloured

pencil on tracing paper. Not signed, dated. 47.5 x 35 cm. Nederlands Documentatiecentrum voor de Bouwkunst, Amsterdam.

92 Apartment Block 2, Spaarndammerplantsoen, Amsterdam (executed in a different form). c. 1914. Graphite and coloured pencil on tracing paper. Not signed or dated. 16.2 x 34.8 cm. Nederlands Documentatiecentrum voor de Bouwkunst, Amsterdam.

93 Apartment Block 2, Spaarndammerplantsoen, Amsterdam. Exterior ornament. c. 1914–16. Graphite and red pencil on tracing paper. Not signed or dated. 28 x 39.4 cm. Nederlands Documentatiecentrum voor de Bouwkunst, Amsterdam.

94 Apartment Block 2, Spaarndammerplantsoen, Amsterdam. Detail of entrance. c. 1914–16. Graphite. Not signed or dated. Nederlands Documentatiecentrum voor de Bouwkunst, Amsterdam.

95 Apartment Block 3, Spaarndammerplantsoen, Amsterdam. Hembrugstraat elevation. c. 1917–20. Graphite and red pencil on tracing paper. Not signed or dated. 15 x 37.5 cm (detail), 17.5 x 68.6 cm (entire sheet). Nederlands Documentatiecentrum voor de Bouwkunst, Amsterdam.

96 Apartment Block 3, Spaarndammerplantsoen, Amsterdam. c. 1917–20. Graphite on tracing paper. Not signed or dated. Nederlands Documentatiecentrum voor de Bouwkunst, Amsterdam.

97 Apartment Block 3, Spaarndammerplantsoen, Amsterdam. Chimney. c. 1917–20. Graphite. Not signed or dated. 22.4 x 30.6 cm. Nederlands Documentatiecentrum voor de Bouwkunst, Amsterdam.

98 Apartment Building, Spaarndammerplantsoen, Amsterdam. Chimney. c. 1918–20. India ink and graphite. Not signed or dated. Nederlands Documentatiecentrum voor de Bouwkunst, Amsterdam.

99 Auction Hall for Flower Sales, Aalsmeer. 1923. Graphite and coloured pencil. Not signed or dated. 20.5 x 46 cm. Nederlands Documentatiecentrum voor de Bouwkunst, Amsterdam.

100 De Hoop Boat Club, Amsterdam. 1922. India ink. Not signed, dated. 13.5 x 37.2 cm. Nederlands Documentatiecentrum voor de Bouwkunst, Amsterdam.

101 De Hoop Boat Club, Amsterdam. 1922. India ink. Signed and dated. 24.4 x 57.4 cm. Nederlands Documentatiecentrum voor de Bouwkunst, Amsterdam.

Pieter Lodewijk Kramer
b. 1881 Amsterdam – d. 1961 Amsterdam. Worked from 1903–13 in the office of Eduard Cuypers. Collaborated with Johan Melchior van der Mey and Michel de Klerk from 1911–16 on the

Scheepvaarthuis, Amsterdam. Designed a great number of bridges for the City of Amsterdam between 1917 and 1952.

102 Bridge over the Binnenamstel, Amsterdam. 1921. Graphite and coloured pencil on tracing paper. Not signed or dated. 29.5 x 99 cm. Nederlands Documentatiecentrum voor de Bouwkunst, Amsterdam.

103 Bridge over the Binnenamstel, Amsterdam. 1921. Graphite and coloured pencil. Not signed or dated. 32.6 x 94 cm. Nederlands Documentatiecentrum voor de Bouwkunst, Amsterdam.

Hendrikus Theodorus Wijdeveld
b. 1885 The Hague. Collaborated with Petrus Josephus Hubertus Cuypers from 1899–1905. 1918–25 Chief Editor of the journal *Wendingen*.

104 Bridge on the Leidseplein, Amsterdam. c. 1920. Graphite on tracing paper. Not signed or dated. 22 x 43 cm. Nederlands Documentaciecentrum voor de Bouwkunst, Amsterdam.

105 Bridge on the Leidseplein, Amsterdam. c. 1920. Graphite on tracing paper. Not signed or dated. 22 x 42.5 cm. Nederlands Documentatiecentrum voor de Bouwkunst, Amsterdam.

106 Large Popular Theatre, Vondelpark, Amsterdam. c. 1919. Charcoal. Not signed or dated. 49 x 66 cm. Nederlands Documentatiecentrum voor de Bouwkunst, Amsterdam.

Willem Kromhout
b. 1864 Amsterdam – d. 1940. Studied from 1878–81 at the Ambachtschool (Trade School), The Hague, followed by evening courses at The Hague Art Academy. Taught from 1897–99 at the Quellinus School, Amsterdam, from 1900–10 at the Rijksnormaalschool voor Tekenonderwijzers, and from 1910–15 at the Academie voor Kunst en Wetenschappen, Rotterdam.

107 Heineken's Brewery, Rotterdam. First design. 1925. Photostat worked over with charcoal. Signed and dated. 50 x 75 cm. Nederlands Documentatiecentrum voor de Bouwkunst, Amsterdam.

Index of names

Photo Credits

Akademie der Künste, Berlin 24, 26–30, 38, 39, 42–51
Bauhaus-Archiv, Berlin 59
Nederlands Documentatiecentrum voor de Bouwkunst, Amsterdam 90–110
Inge + Arved v. d. Ropp, Cologne 34 (top), 36, 41, 88, 89
Staatliche Museen Preußischer Kulturbesitz, Berlin, Kunstbibliothek mit Museum Architektur, Modebild und Graphik-Design 64, 66, 67, 70, 71, 79
Staatsgalerie Stuttgart, Graphische Sammlung 32, 33, 34 (bottom)
Stiftung Deutsche Kinemathek, Berlin 82, 83
Technische Universität Berlin 73, 74, 76, 77
VEB Verlag der Kunst, Dresden 11, 13 (top)
Westfälisches Landesmuseum für Kunst und Kulturgeschichte, Münster 35